THE BOY IN T

'One of the many attractions of this l
older man is able to look back upon his younger self. This is a tribute to both the
writer and, in a sense, to Hillman as a human being... *The Boy in the Green Suit* is
an exquisitely painful book about one of the besetting conditions of modern life:
restlessness... There's an old adage that you can change the scenery but not
yourself. Hillman tells that story with poignancy and warmth'
Australian Book Review

'Hillman's observations of early 1950s family life and the "colony of ruin
that lies in all adult hearts" are particularly poignant. He writes with
an understatement that is deceptive in its simplicity'
Australian Bookseller & Publisher

'The great challenge of all memoirs is to walk the tightrope between personal
reminiscence and stories which resonate far beyond the author and his or
her family and friends. Robert Hillman achieves this balancing act... with a
wonderfully persuasive sense of innocent and endearing daydreaming'
The Sydney Morning Herald

'The book becomes the story of physical and psychic survival, with a sub-plot
around the story of Hillman's father, recreated as a strong and deeply troubled
presence. While it has familiar familial themes, Hillman's complete lack of
sentimentality gives it a punch sometimes lacking in such memoirs. Further,
when the wild ride across the Middle East and parts of south Asia ends,
when the boy is home and the book is closed, readers may find themselves
only just beginning to marvel at the ordeal it describes'
The Australian

'Hillman's resilience alone makes this a memoir worth reading. A childhood
where he was thought to be simple, a mother's desertion and much more, and
yet the person shining through these pages has a great charm and optimism'
The Bulletin, Australia

'It's a wonderful story... Robert Hillman writes about his relationship with his
father and how that came to be, how he came to understand his motivation...
for doing all that travelling, which was really to find love and acceptance'
ABC Radio

the boy in the green suit

an innocent abroad in the middle east

Robert Hillman

summersdale

THE BOY IN THE GREEN SUIT

First published by Scribe Publications in 2003

This edition published in 2005 by Summersdale Publishers Ltd

Summersdale Publishers Ltd
46 West Street
Chichester
West Sussex
PO19 1RP
UK

www.summersdale.com

Printed and bound in Great Britain.

ISBN 1 84024 057 1

It is not our tragedy that we lose our innocence.
It is our duty to do so.
R. P. Blackmur

To Marion

Robert Hillman was born in 1948 and grew up in rural Victoria. He left school at an early age and travelled extensively. He began writing in the early 1980s, publishing short fiction and poetry in literary magazines. His first novel, *A Life of Days*, appeared in 1988, and was followed by *The Hour of Disguise* (1990), *Writing Sparrow Hill* (1996) and *The Deepest Part of the Lake* (2001). After many years of teaching in high schools and university, Robert Hillman now works as a full-time writer. He has three children and lives in Warburton, in Victoria's Yarra Valley.

Contents

 Telephone

EARLY IN 1954, when nothing at all was happening in the rest of Australia, my home town was destroyed. It was neither a sudden nor a natural disaster that brought about the destruction, but the result could not have been more complete if a cyclone had swept down the valley and flattened every house. It left families in mourning and fell like a shroud over the town's vision of its future. Most who experienced the disaster never recovered.

It happened like this.

Into the lazy, green valley in which my home town of Eildon lay came a small army of highly skilled and almost fanatically motivated engineers from America. The year was 1949. The American engineers had been contracted by the government of the state of Victoria to construct an enormous dam on the site of an existing, more modest dam. The Americans were also required to build a power station and a number of ancillary dams. To house the workers who would do all the pick-and-shovel stuff, the Americans extended the existing town, erecting hundreds of homes up and down a grid approximating the design of Manhattan – many streets known only by a number; a few fancy avenues.

The completed town was a masterpiece. The houses were comfortable and attractive. Everything worked as it should. Hot water units never failed; the laundry coppers afforded a washday result that the most modern Maytag could not better; the plumbing was perfect; the sewer system was state of the art. The houses were all built to the one design, but no matter; they looked great. What the Americans had created was a Bauhaus *Siedlung*: a settlement based on inexpensive, functional housing for people who earned their living with the sweat of their brow.

The Americans were geniuses at both work and leisure. My town, unsurprisingly, did not have a golf course; the Americans built one. They built a rifle range, too, and a movie house. Noting the paucity of feast days in the local calendar, the Americans established Halloween, Independence Day and Thanksgiving as important community fêtes. Baseball was introduced as a rival to cricket, and won some converts.

The leisure-time innovations of the Americans were welcomed, but more admired was the sheer vigour with which the Yanks went about entertaining themselves. Rural Australians of the 1950s knew of the relationship between getting pissed and feeling jolly, but not much of the variegation of amusement. When the Americans hired the Progress Hall and staged square dances, the locals loved it. The people of my town might have hired the Progress Hall themselves and whooped it up on a Saturday night, but they hadn't thought of it. The dances organised before the Yanks arrived had been lacklustre.

The pay was terrific, working for the Yanks. An ordinary, unskilled worker could afford things that had been fantasies a few years earlier. A second-hand car came within the financial reach of most. And for each kid, an everyday pair of shoes and a second pair for best. My second pair of shoes thrilled me. When I put them on, I felt that nothing bad could ever happen to me. What my shoes were to me, a black Humber with only thirty thousand miles on the clock was to others, or the soul-deep satisfaction of being able to pay all bills as they arrived.

But as the project drew toward completion, bravado took the place of confidence. Saturday night parties dragged on a little too long. The drunks I met when I woke late at night and wandered down to the kitchen for a drink of water were no longer smiling drunks. They'd left the party in the lounge room to mope. Instead of tousling my hair and commenting on my gorgeous eyelashes (as the lady drunks did), then taking me back to bed for a story from my *Adventure Ahoy!* book of illustrated sea yarns, they glanced at me with empty unconcern and turned away. Denny Holmes, a friend of my dad's, attempted to shoot trout from the town bridge with a .303 at midnight and had to be restrained. Women with Yank lovers aired claims of abandonment. Heartache was everywhere. We thought they loved us, the Yanks, and now they were off to build another dam in Brazil, or Peru, or somewhere. When they left, the gaiety died, the town collapsed. Two thousand jobs became one hundred. My family stayed on.

The community slid into the drabness of the past. Or perhaps it was all to do with contrast. After all, I didn't know the past all that well. But I knew that a meanness, a bitterness, a spiteful ill-will was loose in my house, and in the homes of my friends. Joan Horton no longer tucked her dress into her knickers and drew little faces on her knees with lipstick and made the faces talk to each other as she danced across the living room floor. Horrie Cooper was not interested in pretending to drink his beer through his ear. Parties died out altogether. Former friends became rivals for the few remaining jobs. Wives grew resentful, imagining that their husbands could do more to fashion a future than trapping rabbits in the hills or tapping a nine gallon down at the Progress Hall to discuss the establishment of a Tourism Committee.

Marriages broke down in the same way that the cars of the Yank era chugged to a halt. No money for a new starter motor, no money for a uniform now that the oldest kid had moved on to high school. In my house, the level of bickering increased until it seemed that anything at all could lead to screaming. Or worse than screaming. I came upon strange dramas that cast my parents in roles that could not have frightened me more if the props had included bleeding goats' heads mounted on stakes. My father holding the neck of a broken beer bottle to his own throat, while my mother, perfecting an expression of supreme uninterest, shelled peas at the kitchen table. My mother at the stove, dreamily placing the tip of one finger on the hotplate, flinching and shaking her hand rapidly in the air, then trying another finger, and another. Without knowing what lunatic behaviour of this sort foreshadowed, I knew that something horrible was stalking me.

When I look back on the last days of my parents' marriage, I think of the little colony of ruin that lies in all adult hearts – the lightless place where all that is too ugly or squalid to face is sent, as lepers were once hidden away. I see that the colony had spread, had invaded the mainland. I looked to my sister

Marion, years older than me, for some relief. But her distress was even worse than mine. The fear that was stalking me had already overtaken her.

My mother left. She went dressed in a beautiful red overcoat, one I had always admired. She carried a large suitcase. My sister was on the high school bus to Alexandra. I had been told to take myself to the primary school. I was in Bubs, and normally my mother would walk me to school. I didn't want to leave. I loitered, and was permitted to loiter. I sat on the front step and watched my mother walk down the street, leaning to one side to balance the heavy suitcase. I went back into the house and stared at the letter she had left on the telephone table for my father. I picked it up. It felt too light in its white envelope to mean anything. Then I went to school, hoping that my mother would be there, believing that she would. I was baffled to find that she wasn't.

In the years that followed my mother's departure, my bafflement grew. She made no contact with me or my sister or my father. I believed that she had gone to America with all her square-dance dresses and was living in Chicago or Texas and was having a great time, twirling on the toes of her shoes as she used to and making her petticoats lift and swell. (This morose reverie turned out to be a close approximation of the truth.)

I associated the dreariness of the town with my mother's absence. My most pressing concern became the obstinate ordinariness of the town, and the life it offered me. The paradise years, when a crowd of cheerful people from America had made my mother and father joyful, had convinced me that great happiness was my due and my destiny. I was no worse off in my small town than any other child in any other small Australian town. But I believed in paradise. My paradise altered with my age. It was a place where an enormous banquet table afforded me a fabulous choice of breakfast cereals – in the days of skinny pay packets for my father and stale bread soaked in watery milk for breakfast. It became the most magnificent library in the world when I discovered the miracles that writers could conjure in books. It was a green paddock where my mother and father set up a picnic on a plaid blanket and invited my sister and me to sit on their laps while they whispered endearments into our ears. That version owed something to a television advertisement for Tarax lemonade, I think.

My Eden projects were probably more obsessive than those of other kids, though hardly unique. Every child fashions versions of paradise. But in my case, no correctives were offered. My sister left the town for the city. My father, a busy fantasist himself, only occasionally registered that I was off the track and into the mulga.

One evening, after my father had finished his day's work clearing drains for the shire council, we went out into the hills in his old Morris van to gather firewood. We did this twice a week in winter. We ended up not far from one of my little Edens. I thought I would show it to him. I led the way to the mouth of an abandoned gold mine – one of a number of old mines tunnelled by misinformed prospectors in the early 1900s. My father carried the Tilley lamp we used when chopping wood in the evenings.

Some way into the dark mine, after a number of turns, we came to my project. I had set up a makeshift table, and on the table rested the handpiece of a telephone with a short length of flex attached. I'd found it at the town tip. Two candles stood in the necks of tomato sauce bottles, one each side of the telephone. I lit the candles then explained to my father, who looked perplexed, that I came here to make telephone calls, sometimes with the candles burning, sometimes in the dark. 'Who to?' my father wanted to know, more worried now. 'Oh,' I said, 'to anyone.' And I added – it seemed important to do so – that the calls were pretend calls. 'Yeah, but who to?' my father persisted. 'Oh, to you, to Marion, to Mum.' My father's face, bathed a pale yellow in the candle light, took on an expression of concern. 'Don't do this any more,' he said, and led me out of the mine. In the fading evening light, he said again, 'Don't do this any more, understand?'

I didn't do it any more. Instead, I began searching for lost cities, ready-made Edens, concealed in the hills. I didn't go to the gold mine again. The telephone handpiece may still be exactly where I left it. I could go and check, if I wished. I could take my own children with me. But I won't go. For one thing, attempting to persuade your children that you yourself had a childhood is too algebraic for kids. For another, I wish to believe that the telephone *does* remain where I left it all those years ago, its length of flex connected to nothing.

Whenever I used that telephone, I conjured the listener. I heard the voice at the other end. I heard sounds of encouragement. I told stories to the listener, stories of fact, stories of myself, what was happening at school, at home. I gave football scores, gave an account of the death of a friend who had drowned in the lake, offered summaries of the books I was reading. It comforted me to tell the stories.

The telephone, undisturbed, sits on a tea chest deep in the gold mine. The candles are burning. I have a cut lunch, a cask of cheap lambrusco, a packet of cigarettes. The silence is so intense that I can hear the sound that flame makes as it consumes a wick. I've taken a cigarette from the packet and I'm leaning forward on my knees to ignite its tip.

I am as ready as I will ever be.

I pick up the telephone.

 Butcher Shop

ON A GREEN island across the seas, naked women, tall and supple, laboured in the fields of a tea plantation – or so it was said. But it was later said that the women were not entirely naked. They wore bright sarongs tied at the waist. A few other details were also changed. I began to fear that the women would turn out not to be naked at all. It was important to me that the description of their breasts as 'full, very full' should not be altered. Their smiles flashed an invitation. 'Kiss me. I am yours, blue-eyed Aussie soldier, visitor to our shores. Kiss me, and my sister, too.'

I came to know of these generous women when I was eleven years old. My father told me about them. He'd met them during the war, somewhere in the Islands. Successive episodes of his encounters with them provided more intimacy. 'My Aussie darling,' they said as they undressed him. On occasion, three sisters would vie for his attention. They were always sisters, never just friends. Sequential sexual adventures with women related by blood seemed to gee my father up.

The story of the bare-breasted women was the most wonderful story I'd ever heard. But I was careful, always, to make sure that my attention did not betray anything lickerish.

That would have been the end of the stories. I looked interested, I smiled, I sometimes laughed. But I never embarrassed my father, never said, 'Wow!' or, 'Boy oh boy!' My expression said, 'Thanks Dad, fascinating stuff.' Nothing more. He was educating me, he allowed himself to believe. I was eleven. I needed to hear stories like this.

With fiction, the audience is everything. The idea of authors writing to please themselves and no one else has always seemed crazy to me. You write for people who are just a little bit more difficult to please than yourself. My father's fictions (as they surely were) took proper account of his audience. I was a little more difficult to please than he. I liked detail, and he gave me detail. One of the women had a silver filling in her tooth. (A worker on a tea plantation?) Another played the mandolin while her sister sang. His story-telling manner was nonchalant, yet conscientious. We would be fishing down on the river or up at the lake. He always sniffed twice before he began, as if inhaling the little extra air needed to prepare his narrative voice. 'I dunno if you should be hearing this,' he would say, and then he would tell me. I loved him for it. I loved the lies. If none of this happened to my father, I thought, it must have happened to someone.

Any child can pick up a yarn that draws together fragments of daydream, threads of ambition, only to find much later that it has become the initial paragraph of a life story. Those first few lines of story may determine who you marry – your choice puzzling those who know you. They may reverberate when you choose the names for your children, find yourself in bed with your best friend's wife, invent an amazing system of airborne travel, shoot yourself. The opening paragraph will act as more than words, as a wax holding together the feathers of homemade wings. The green island of absurdly complaisant women became the opening of my story, which is a new version of my father's story. Passing on your genes is said to be a formidable imperative of species. To pass on your fantasies, to have your children act out a new and possibly improved version of the yarn of your life, might constitute a more subtle tactic in the quest for immortality.

I was fifteen in 1963, and dim. I should go further and say that even amongst a crowd of dim fifteen year olds, I would have stood out. I had left school early, more or less because my father had expected that I would. He saw no virtue in education beyond the subsistence level. I could read and write – what more did I want? What I wanted had only partly formed in my mind at that time, but through the mist I could make out an edenic island, white sand, palm trees, small but well-made huts grouped beneath the trees and, nearby, a library. The library was important. I enjoyed reading, but on the island, so far as I could tell, it would be difficult for me to earn much of an income for the purchase of books. I would probably have to be kept as a type of pet by the beautiful and salacious women who were the only other inhabitants of the island – or the only ones I cared to bring into slightly sharper focus. But that was in the future.

For the time being, my father had accepted a job for me, offered in the pub by Bertie Fisher, the butcher in my home town. I was to become Bertie's apprentice.

'You've got to do *something*, y' know,' my father explained. 'You've got to do *something* for a living.'

'I know.'

'Well, what's the matter with it? It's a good job. Make money as a butcher.'

My sister Marion, now living in the city, had gone to work at the age of fourteen. My father had always spoken proudly of her initiative. It was important that I measured up to my sister, gave my father equal cause for pride.

'Okay,' I said.

My father had lived through the Great Depression. Employment to him, and to every other male Australian of his class and generation, was victory. He didn't trust life or anything about it, but if you had a job, you'd had a win. It wasn't possible for him to study me for a minute or two, with all his prejudices put aside, and ask himself if this slight and dozy boy with pink cheeks and a girl's eyelashes could comfortably take his place behind a zinc counter in a striped apron. It was a good job. It was a victory.

I was worried about Bertie, more than anything else. The island – well, I would still get to the island. But Bertie was a tough bastard, that was what everybody said, and he scared me. He was short and ugly with a powerful chest and over-developed forearms. His nose looked as if it had been chewed by something – human, animal, machine – then partly repaired. It tapered to an unnaturally flat tip. It was his hands that properly frightened me. He could lift things with just one of his huge, club-like fists that most people would struggle to hoist with two. He would take hold of a pig's carcass and toss it along the butchering slab with a nonchalant flick, and once I watched him sink a spade into a pile of offal, lift it horizontal with a single hand (he had a Lucky Strike in the other), study the greyish-pink mass for a minute or more, then heave it into the copper.

I worked in the backyard of the butcher shop most of the time. The furnace and copper were kept there. I would load offal and offcuts into the copper, rendering it all down to lard. The stink was awful. I could gaze up to the hills that circled the town, and set my soul on routes of escape. The near hills had been cleared root and stump by squatters in the old days, and in the spring glowed green in the sunlight. In summer they took on a tawny wheatfield colour. Beyond, the mountains climbed into the sky. I had roamed those hills, climbed the mountains. I knew of cool, shaded valleys bedded with moss and ferns.

Staring up at the hills from the backyard of the butcher's shop while the offal boiled, I dreamed of the special colony I hoped one day to found up there. The colony would accept women almost exclusively. And not just any women. I was thinking of maybe a dozen women, all like Jenny Macrae, a soft, blowsy girl from my fourth-form class with yellow hair and cushiony breasts and lips that always looked slightly bruised. Other pretty girls, teased by boys at school, would respond by dobbing to Mrs Spencer, who looked on all males as swamp life. Spence would push a boy against a wall and savage him until tears dampened his cheeks. 'If you've got something to say to that lass, you say it like a *gentleman*. Do you understand what a gentleman is? Of course you don't, it's a mystery to you, you ugly little chap.' But Jenny, taunted, would call musically over her shoulder, 'Anus face!', not with much malice, and go on her way.

I never hoped for a dozen copies of Jenny in my colony. I hoped for mature women – older versions of her. I never asked myself just why twelve beautiful women, mature and experienced, would wish to live in a secluded valley with a fifteen-year-old butcher's apprentice. In any case, I didn't wish to spend a great deal of time with the colony women. I wanted to have sex with each of them a few times a day, then ride my bike into town and go fishing with my friends, or maybe kick a football around. During my recreation time – a large part of each day – the women would be free to please themselves. They might cook, or read magazines, for example.

From the back of the shop, I could hear Bertie singing. He had a sweet tenor voice with a nice quaver. He sang Hank Williams's songs: 'Your Cheatin' Heart', 'Jambalaya', 'Hey, Good Lookin''. He was cheerful, as most butchers are, and kept up an effortless banter with the customers:

'Six mid-loin mutton, no problem with that at all.'

'Trim the fat, Bertie, but not too much.'

'Be capable of that, Dulce.'

'And some mince. Not too fine. Don't like it too fine.'

'Sounds reasonable, Dulce. Anything reasonable, I'm happy to do.'

'Too fine, it falls to bits.'

'Wouldn't want that. Wouldn't want your rissoles all over the place, Dulce.'

Bertie employed a second butcher, Eric, an Aboriginal with a curious handicap for a man who'd chosen to cut up animals for a living: he sickened at the sight of blood. The pink and red of the meat didn't trouble him, but blood on the move made his knees turn to jelly. He must have kept this weakness

22

to himself when he was offered the job, because I was in the shop to hear Bertie complain of the extra work that Eric had loaded on him.

'Got a cow out at Taggerty to pick up tomorra. Y'can do that, hey?'

'Load it on the truck for yuh, bring it back here,' Eric apologised.

'What the fuck's the good of a cow to me? I want it shot, I want it chopped!'

'Can't do that, mate.'

'Why fuckin' can't yuh?'

'Don't like it. Never have.'

Eric made up for his squeamishness by taking a conscientious role in my education as a butcher. He'd bring me in from the copper to demonstrate the skill of the sausage maker.

'Y' know what you call this, Bobby?'

'Skin?'

'Yeah, it's skin orright, it's skin when it's on y' sausage. But it's called "casing" when y' take it outa the box. "Casing", right?'

'Casing,' I repeated.

'Right. Now, y' slip y' casing over this thing here, y' tap. Y' call it the "tap". Right? Whadda we call it?'

'The tap,' I said.

'Now, y' mince's inside here, y' sausage mince. Put what y' like in there, mince it up, out it comes from the tap into the casing. Y' don't let him run f' too long. Don't wanna snag a mile long, hey? Don't want that, do we? So whadda we do with him?'

'Make it into smaller sausages?'

'Good! Good on yuh, Bobby! Make it into smaller snags. Twist it here, here, here, make a string of 'em. That's how y' make y' sausages. Wanna have a go?'

'No,' I said.

''Course y' do! Have a go!'

My father had felt it his duty to tell Bertie that I was 'a bit vague'. I was standing beside him when he gave out this information, and I remember that he lowered his voice, and seemed embarrassed. Anything about a person that reduced his value to an employer made my father uncomfortable. He went on to tell Bertie that I might need a boot up the arse occasionally. I was shocked to hear him say that, because he never laid much of a hand on me himself. Some of my friends fared much worse. I noticed that whenever I was chastised for daydreaming, for not paying attention to the here-and-now, there was always a further suggestion of shiftiness, as if my daydreams were subversive.

'Full of secrets, aren't we?' my stepmother would say, one eyebrow raised. 'You don't fool me.'

'I'm not trying to fool you.'

'Yes you are. Yes you are. But it doesn't work with me.'

Gwen had developed a smug vigilance whenever she was alone with me, giving me sidelong looks and smiling quietly. It was as if she were saying, 'Right, there's no one here for you to work your way around, only canny old me – so don't try anything.' She had become suspicious of me since I'd revealed that the slightly supercilious Adam Cartwright was my favourite character on *Bonanza* – a hugely popular television western.

'Yes, well you would, wouldn't you?' Gwen jeered. 'Moody, just like you. Hey, Frank! Who do you thing Bobby likes best? Adam!'

'Adam! Jesus!'

My father had just come in from the kitchen. He'd been making the tea during the ad break.

'Sneaky,' said Gwen. 'Just like Bobby.'

'I'm not sneaky!'

'Yes you are! You're a sly little bugger, the way you get those blanks.'

Gwen was referring to *Scrabble*. She was bitter. It meant a great deal to her, winning at *Scrabble*. Her entire recreational life was devoted to *Scrabble*, crosswords, detective stories and fishing. She required an adversary. When she read, she had to discover the killer before the author revealed the name. When she fished, she would gloat for days over landing a trout. She believed that trout were sly, too. The entire population of the town was divided between the disingenuous and the candid, so far as she was concerned.

I don't think Bertie believed that I was sly. I don't think he believed that I had the brains for it. Certainly he took no pains to conceal his political feints and dodges from me. For the butcher's shop was also the unofficial headquarters of the town's conservatives. Joe Naylor, who owned almost all the land from the Goulburn River to the mountains, would call in a couple of times a week to nut out shire council strategy with Bertie. Neither Joe nor Bertie sat on the council, but they controlled it through stooges. They spoke of their puppets with contempt, despising them, so far as I could tell, even more than they did their Labor enemies. I was a communist. The politics of the council interested me.

Whenever Joe lumbered into the shop, I'd find myself something to do not too far away. Bertie and Joe, each side of the counter, leaned toward each other over the spread sheets of newspaper used for wrapping. Joe made me think of an ancient turtle, his head drawn into his shoulders, his face blotched with dark melanoma in some places and bleached white in others. Wrinkled yellow crescents hung under his eyes. While he was talking with Bertie, his head would thrust forward as if spying out opportunities for malice, then draw back. I considered both Bertie and Joe my political enemies. My acts of subversion extended to writing 'MARX' in red crayon on the inside of the coarse, white butcher's paper I used when wrapping orders of sausages.

Eric, watching me as I stirred the offal in the boiler one morning, gave his head a worried shake. I glanced away, then looked back, and Eric still seemed worried.

'Hey, Bobby, y' wanna do this for a livin'? Y' don't, do yuh?'

'It's okay,' I said.

'Yeah, but y' oughta go to school. What y' doin' here, Bobby?'

'I left school,' I said, vaguely ashamed.

'Y' oughtn'a. Y' oughtn'a left school. Fuckin', y' don't wanna do this all y' life, Bob.'

'I'm going to an island,' I said. 'I'm saving up.'

'Island? What island?'

'The Seychelles,' I said.

'Seychelles? Where the fuck's that, the Seychelles?'

I knew where the Seychelles were. They basked in the Indian Ocean off Mombasa. I imagined the Seychelles to correspond in every feature to the green island of my daydreams. I saw myself stretched out on the yellow sands of the Seychelles beaches. My body would fill with warmth, like an apricot ripening on a bough. I would wear a sarong. My father had told me that both women and men wore sarongs on such islands. Mine would be blue and yellow, the colours of the sky and sand. The native woman who was my special love (I would call her Jenny, with her consent, though her native name would be quite different, something like Ooguma) would stroll down every so often to ask if I were ready to make love in our grass hut. I might lazily reply that I would be ready in another hour or so. I would say this gently, not carelessly, for the fact was that I loved Jenny/Ooguma and, even more importantly, she loved me. Jenny/Ooguma's love for me was an innovation in my daydreams. Previously, I had only required her to desire me.

I didn't mention any of this to Eric. His worried look frayed the edges of my daydream. I realised that he was not simply worried about my future as a butcher; he was worried about my whole life. He had more to go on than the voyage to the Seychelles. Once when I was stirring the offal in the boiler he had overheard me calling, for an imaginary radio audience, the magnificent over that saw me bring up the twenty runs I needed for my century in a deciding Ashes test. The intensity of my call, and perhaps also the insistence on verisimilitude, would have troubled him a fair bit. (I had described the bowler as 'swarthy in appearance' – unusual for an Englishman, but the word appealed to me.)

I was not entirely insane, but a boy who relies too much on the imagination to decorate the bare halls of his life is in danger of seeming so. It requires steely handling, imagination, and I was just barely in control at fifteen. Eric had caught me in only a mild mood of escapism. What if he'd studied me playing 'Two Goals Down and Ten Minutes to the Siren' – my favourite game of all? I played that game in the backyard of an empty house in Fourth Street. Thirty-six individual surfaces – chimney, fences, garage, walls, verandah – became the players of the two Australian Rules teams that took part in the game. My role was to bring all these inanimate surfaces to life by racing around and kicking a tennis ball to the players, then catching the ball when it rebounded. I also provided the commentary, preserving the immortal clichés of Saturday afternoon radio calls on 3UZ, 3DB, 3KZ. Gavin Hallet, a friend of my father's, stopped to watch me one time. I was encouraged by the smile on his face to keep playing – he apparently didn't see anything odd in the game. But he later asked my father if I was 'all there', and I could tell by the way my father reported this that he wanted reassurance.

My great ally in my battle for freedom from the town and the life it could offer me was my incompetence. I did everything badly. My sausages came out of the machine too long or too short, lumpy or leaky. And without knowing how it happened, I always managed to coat myself in mince. 'You've got ten bob to wash off that friggin' apron,' Bertie would tell me. My incompetence – as a butcher's apprentice and in every other situation – grieved my father deeply. He was a legendary worker in my town and could turn his hand to anything manual or mechanical with complete success. He had a deft touch, too, so that his success never appeared laboured. I watched in wonder once as he calmly repaired the clutch of our Morris, coolly selecting each piece of the puzzle that lay spread around him until the whole apparatus was rebuilt and re-installed. It worked perfectly, though everything he'd done had been based on a few brief instructions from the garage mechanic, Arnie Wold. At such times my love for him developed a fine, well-oiled hum. He would glance across at me, smile, and with that smile forgive the whole catalogue of my failures.

It was a pity that I disappointed my father so consistently, because I doubt anyone more admired him. And I admired him in the way he wanted to be admired. Pencil-thin as I was, and too pretty for a boy, I was thrilled by the sheer masculinity of my father. He had a graceful, laconic physicality. When he went to work with an axe on a pile of wood, fat chips of redgum flew through the air and the muscles of his forearms bulged and glistened. Every so often he stopped to catch his breath, and he'd grin at me and wink, light up a Temple Bar. It was best for me to remain silent, just express my awe with my wide-open eyes. I mucked it all up one day when I told him he looked 'indomitable'. He grunted, just barely accepting the compliment.

I was forever trying to impress my father in the only possible way that I could impress him – by giving him evidence of my willingness to work hard. Once I'd reached the age of ten, he took me with him on weekend jobs he'd pick up all over the district. The extra work was important. Like most working-class families in the early 'sixties, we were always short, always trying to sniff out the extra two or three pounds that stood between worry and a clear run for a few weeks. The job might be anything – clearing bracken and ti-tree for the cockies; reroofing a bungalow with iron; clearing drains down at the caravan park. A new source of work came along when people with money from Melbourne began building weekenders on land around the more remote inlets of the huge lake above the town. It was always cash-in-hand work, the price rapidly negotiated in mutters down in the shopping centre. Listening in, I'd hope for work arduous enough to let me show my mettle, but not so hard that it left me knackered.

'Been told you'd be right for a day's work, Frank.'

'Yeah, could be. What's the job?'

'Laying concrete.'

'Have to be cash in hand.'

'Too right.'

'What's it paying?'

'Dunno. Say fifteen bob an hour? Might take you five, six hours?'

'Make it eighteen bob, won't go over five hours.'

And then, when the man had departed: 'Get you to help me, Bobby.'

'Okay.'

'Four and a half quid. We'll tell Gwen three, okay? Ten bob for you, an extra quid for me. You got that?'

'Yep.'

I think there must have been a network of deceit amongst working men all over Australia at that time. Because it was not just my father who kept a bit back from the money he made, but all of his mates. They backed each other up. If my father and two mates had taken on a job, an agreement was made about the amount they'd report to their wives. Without a bit held back, there'd be no beer at the end of the job, no bet with the SP bookie, no new oil filter for the car – no reward for the sweat and toil. My father and all the other fathers I knew feared or hated their wives and looked on them as wardens. The hostility was always there, with the wives' eyes permanently narrowed, and a soft, spaniel-ish, wounded expression in the husbands' eyes. The women were battling on their children's behalf: shoes to replace a pair that wouldn't see out another fortnight, trip to the dentist, football boots promised for a couple of years now. But if a little windfall came along – God knows from where – all the spite and suspicion evaporated. Husbands and wives smiled, goodwill returned, passably generous things were said by each about the other.

As for my pay, I would never see that. I would have preferred my father to say, 'Can't pay you anything, sorry.' It embarrassed me to hear my father make these promises he had no intention of keeping. Of course, he would have hated to admit that the promise was fantasy. He wanted to pay me. It wasn't miserliness that made it impossible. In any case, I was glad of the money that came into the household from these occasional jobs. The money brought peace.

The regular arguments of my father and stepmother often made me doubt my sanity. For they despised each other with a hatred that was inexhaustible. Each had a catalogue of grievances so detailed and cross-referenced that any accusation would instantly be countered by an accusation from the same section of a parallel list. They would circle each other in the kitchen like a pair of enraged baboons, leaning forward from the waist with teeth bared. Anything that could wound was used. Neither was capable of restraint when the anger was strong enough – not even the presence of me or my two stepsisters. Listening, I would wince when one of them left an opening for the other, certain of what would happen. A gloating look, the advantage seized, then venomous words would hiss from a crooked mouth.

My stepmother's most deadly line of attack had to do with why my mother left my father – his 'stinking temper'; he 'couldn't hold his liquor any better than a kid'. Once on top, she was relentless: 'What would make a woman do that, run off and leave two kids behind? Jesus, she must have hated you, Frank, you must have made her life a living hell.' My father would scream that she was a slut, but that only made Gwen laugh.

At his worst, he would menace her with the story of her younger son's death in a car crash a few years earlier, telling her that Jeffrey was better off dead than growing up with a mother like her. When he had her on her knees, he would torment her with the sort of cruelty you would normally associate with the torture chamber. Since it was he who had dragged her dead son from the wreck – and me, with just a few cuts – he was in a position to describe the boy's horrible disfigurement, and threatened to do so, toying with her until she screamed in pain. On most days, my stepmother treated me with affection and humour, but my father's taunts could so derange her that she would cry out in despair, 'Why couldn't it have been Bobby! Why couldn't it have been him!' In a fit of melodrama, my father once held a carving knife across my throat, daring my stepmother to repeat what she'd said. 'I'll take his fucking head off for you – is that what you want?' I wasn't frightened; only ashamed for myself and my father.

Later, he would regret his temper, but the regret could only be borne if he was drunk, and that would start a whole new round of arguments.

I must have decided without quite realising it that six weeks would just about do me at Bertie's. Once those six weeks were up, the urge to reach the Island harped in my head every hour of the day. My town seemed so exhausted of novelty that it existed as components – as if I had taken it apart and put it back together countless times. There were its ordered rows of houses, the creek, High Street, the shopping centre, the oval, the Progress Hall, the Catholic church on top of the hill, the Presbyterian at the bottom of Eighth Street, the old bridge, the new bridge, the river, the lake, the spillway, the dam wall, the pastured hills, the mountains.

All were saturated with experience: fishing in the Goulburn, yabbying in ponds with the soft, greyish-yellow mud oozing up through my toes, riding my bike down Skyline Road with my eyes shut, opening a gash in my head when I crashed, persuading an adorably ripe cousin to kiss me open-mouthed in a bush hut we'd made, collecting books and magazines from the tip, swimming languidly a mile or more across the lake, descending abandoned mine shafts with my back against one wall and my feet against the other, watching my father cast a spinner into the seething white water below the power house, walking dazed and wretched in no direction and every direction when my mother left, forming a club with my friends dedicated to communism, murder and the fleecing of the rich. The town could absorb no more of me.

So it must be the Seychelles. But before the Seychelles, Melbourne. I would need a job, maybe as a steeplejack, maybe as a motor mechanic (I'd seen my father rebuild that clutch, after all), or maybe – yes, maybe this, right here on the sheet of newspaper in which I was wrapping a customer's order: Situations Vacant, Junior Sales Assistants, Ladies' Shoes, *The Myer Emporium*, Bourke Street, Melbourne.

MY ABANDONED FATHER enjoys a good deal of sympathy from men and women alike. Everywhere he goes, his mates slap a hand on his shoulder and shake their heads. *'You wouldn't fucking read about it, Frank. Can't fathom a woman doing a thing like that.'* And from the women: *'She's only kidding herself, Frank. Only kidding herself. Think she's not going to regret this? Don't make me laugh.'*

Supported in this way, my father recovers. He finds the money to purchase a small Singer runabout with a fold-down roof, very perky. He begins to make trips to Melbourne, dashing along the twisting road that runs through Taggerty and Narbethong and over the Black Spur. He takes my sister Marion with him. Now that my mother is gone, my sister at fifteen is the prettiest girl in town, adored by everyone, but also the most wretched. She cries herself sick. The trips to Melbourne cheer her up. My father buys her gorgeous dresses in the city shops (with borrowed money) and takes her to shows at Festival Hall. She carries back souvenir programs that flabbergast me. Johnny Ray, Frank Sinatra, Guy Mitchell — legendary people.

Whenever my father and sister dash off to Melbourne, they make sure they visit the Myer Emporium. My sister cuddles me and whispers in my ear all that she has seen in the wonderful store. One day, she says, I will go with her and Dad. Oh, I won't believe what I will see! Oh, Bobby, Bobby — the cafeteria has everything, just everything, and you can walk along with a tray and you can just choose whatever you want, I mean whatever you want! And there's so many departments, which is why it's called a department store, see, and *everything*, just absolutely *everything* is there, you can't even *believe* it when you see it, just *truly*, Bobby, just true true *truly*!

I stay with a childless Polish couple while Dad and Marion are away. I have never met them before. I know that they are not amongst my father's friends. They treat me with a grave and unfailing kindness, but rarely speak to me. I am baffled. I ask myself, in a blurry way, whether this is a normal thing. Mum there one day, gone the next, suitcase, red coat; Dad and Marion disappearing in the little blue Singer and returning with tales of a distant paradise, a store made up of departments; a couple of peculiar old people dressed in humourless grey left weirdly watching over me.

I am bedded down by the Polish couple in a painstakingly constructed nursery, bunny rabbits running in a frieze around the wall, a strange, foreign-looking cot. The brawny, gentle hand of the Polish wife strokes my hair, tears finding a course down her cheeks. Baffling.

Back home, an argument breaks out. I'm in my own bedroom without bunny rabbits, without the cot and the snuggly blue blanket. My father and sister are hissing in the passage. The words I pick up alarm me. 'Yes, but he'll be *lonely*, oh he will, Dad, he *will*, I promise you he'll be lonely...'

Twenty years pass before this makes sense. Something jolts a cobwebby old file in my brain's archives, the papers spill, I stoop to pick them up and find myself studying those words: '... oh he will, Dad, he *will*, I promise you...' My sister explains, wrongly judging me old enough at twenty-seven to be placed in possession of the facts. It had been intended that the Polish couple would adopt me. I don't know how. But Marion wouldn't hear of it, and my father backed down.

 Emporium

I WORE A grey dustcoat at Myers rather than a striped butcher's apron, but looked no more at home in it. The apron had reached to my ankles; the dustcoat hung on me like a blanket on a famished refugee. And because the department store was full of mirrors, I could not go anywhere without catching sight of myself. I shrank in horror from my appearance. Even for a fantasist, there is a critical point at which conviction wilts. I could make myself believe that a slight boy of fifteen without any accomplishment could have a devastating impact on the women of the green island. But I could not believe in the figure reflected in the mirrors of the emporium.

Perhaps I should think of a more ascetic career, concentrate more on the spirit. The life of a monk, for instance. I had recently read a slender book about a man who approached enlightenment by practising archery under the tutelage of a Zen monk. He had been told to desist from aiming his arrow. The arrow would find the target by itself. Breathing exercises were an important part of learning to strike a target by not aiming. Whenever I caught my reflection and felt my heart wince, I hurried to a secret place I'd located in the upstairs loft of the ladies' slipper department – to practise my breathing, surrounded by cobwebs and a mist of peppery dust.

It was not only the mirrors that menaced me. The store itself was so vast, so busy, that I felt as if I were locked in a dangerous machine that might at any moment seize and crush me. I was told by a supervisor to take slippers to a location on the sixth floor, where they would be photographed for a newspaper ad. I searched hopelessly for the lifts, then tried the escalators, and ended up in the kitchen of one of the store's cafeterias, being shouted at by bad-tempered men pushing trolleys loaded with plates. Finally, a tall, masterful woman in a smart black suit put a hand on my shoulder and guided me to a quiet corner. She took out a handkerchief and dabbed at my eyes.

'What's wrong, precious puss? What's the matter?'

I showed her the slippers and spoke of photographs.

'I'll take you,' she said.

She guided me with what seemed magical ease along corridors and up flights of stairs to a door marked 'Keep Out'. I never saw the woman again, but pictured her in my mind for weeks afterwards. In one comforting drama, she waited for me in Little Lonsdale Street, once again put her hand on my shoulder, took me home and, after a roast dinner, we agreed to marry.

The city outside the emporium was even more terrifying than the store itself. I didn't understand how it worked. The hurtling pedestrians, the rowdy trams, the glowering buildings – how was it that everyone knew what to do, where to go, where to stop, where to turn? I could master only the one, dogged route from Myers to Flinders Street Station. Once on platform 4, I knew to catch the Frankston train, and that was all. If the train were rescheduled and sent to another platform, I became ill with fear. I did not see anyone else who suffered in the way that I did. I believed that a certain code allowed people to negotiate the crush and bustle – something learned in school maybe, on a day that I was wagging. I didn't have the code. I understood nothing.

Once I'd reached my tiny flat in the backyard of a silent suburban home in Frankston (the house and flat were owned by Mrs Timms, a tiny, aged woman with a green plastic eye-patch) I would go to bed fully clothed with a tin of Tom Piper Braised Steak and Vegetables, and eat it cold while reading *Time* and *Life* and various novels from the library. When I went to the bathroom at the back of the house, Mrs Timms would silently appear behind me and hiss something that it took me months to work out. She was saying, 'Easy with the left hand' – meaning, use very little of the hot water, the hot water tap being located on the left of the sink. I thought she was telling some sort of insane joke. I would laugh, my mouth full of toothpaste, and wish devoutly that Mrs Timms would die in the night so that I could bury her in the backyard and never have to see her again.

The ladies' slipper department was run by a lugubrious alcoholic, Vince, who spent most of the working day down the road at the Kilkenny Inn, appearing now and again to shout at Georgie and Nadia, who were the department's real managers. Georgie and Nadia took no notice of anything Vince said, refusing even to reply. Vince, needing an ally, would take me out the back and whinge about 'those two cunts' who were ruining everything for the rest of us. Then he would sigh and fiddle around with invoices for a few minutes, muttering gloomily, 'Breaks your heart, breaks your fucking heart!'

Nadia, a Christian from Delhi, had a particular horror of drunkards, and wondered aloud in a chirping little voice why the laws did not make more of an example of men like Vince. 'I would have him put through the wringer, my very word, over and over if necessary!' But I was comfortable with Vince. My home town had been full of drunks.

Georgie, like Eric back at Bertie's, took an interest in my unfitness for employment and asked me why I'd left school. Her concern took the form of a worried interview, commenced and deferred and recommenced over my whole six months in ladies' slippers. She would take me out behind the stock shelves, light up an unfiltered Chesterfield and question me, pausing regularly to pick pieces of tobacco off the tip of her tongue.

'Now, love, what did your mum say when you left school? Wasn't pleased, was she?'

'She didn't mind.'

'Yeah, I'll bet. You shoulda gone on and got a good job. Solicitor. D'you think they don't make money, solicitors! Or a bank manager. What do you like doing?'

'Reading.'

'See? You coulda been a librarian! Whoops, gotta go, getting busy out there. Put those blue shufflers on the big table near the moccasins.'

Thudding home on the train through the gloom of winter, I began to feel that something either wonderful or terrible must soon happen to me. This was not life. This was not the green island. My yearning for the marvellous and magical reached such a pitch that I had to bite the collar of my duffle coat to prevent myself weeping before the blank faces of my fellow passengers. Once I reached my station I followed a familiar route through dreary streets and across an ill-tended park, where a pair of desperate lovers regularly wrestled on a bench under struggling black wattles and lilly-pillys. I crept into my flat to avoid the whispery welcome from Mrs Timms, and went to work with oil paints on oblongs of Masonite, creating the sort of portraits that are offered in evidence by doctors seeking certification for a worrying patient.

One day at work, I thought up a plan. Wandering the out-of-the-way and off-limits areas of the Myer Emporium in a dazed and miserable state, I came upon a huge coil of rope stored behind a door that gave access to the roof. If you walked across the roof, you could gaze down past the huge clock to the hurly-burly of Bourke Street seven floors below. What a lark, I thought, and how famous it would make me if I were to scale down the face of the building on that rope. How the shoppers and pedestrians and office workers would cheer! 'Look at that bold lad!' they would cry. 'By God, they don't make them like that any more!' I imagined women in the crowd folding their hands over their hearts in silent prayer for my safety. Yes, it was the answer. Later, the green island would provide a more complete answer but, just for now, a hike down the front of Myers would act as a tonic, get me into the newspapers, and would certainly delight all my friends back in Eildon.

I planned the descent carefully. I bought gloves to work with me, to help me grip the rope. I was happy. I made my way to the roof exit, hovered over the rope for a few moments – then the door opened and a man in a very senior-looking blue dustcoat demanded to know what I thought I was doing. 'Nothing,' I said. 'Well, get back to where you belong!' he bawled – and I did.

A week later I bought a typewriter and a cricket bat. The purchase of the cricket bat fulfilled a lifelong dream, but was of no other use to me. I stood it in the corner of the one room that comprised my flat, and stared at it. The typewriter was more useful. I wrote short stories on it. The stories were inspired by my reading of Hemingway and Chekhov. One of the Hemingwayesque stories began, 'She was beautiful. Johnson had to admit it. She was beautiful and tall and her hair was the gold of sawdust from a freshly sawn log of spruce.' The Chekhovian stories were more complex. The characters spoke a lot about their disappointments. I set the stories in Russia, usually in Moscow. Not knowing anything about Moscow, I was forced to make up names for streets and local sites of interest. I named the main street Raskalnikov Street. The stories all ended with one or more of the main characters attempting suicide.

Writing the stories was exciting. It seemed obvious that I would one day win the Nobel Prize for Literature, and I began to think about the house I would need to properly accommodate the cup. I had got the idea that the Nobel Prize winner was given a big gold cup. Perhaps I would buy a crystal cabinet to display it. In all the households that I knew intimately, a crystal cabinet stood in one corner of the living room. Items that were 'too good' for regular use were stored in the cabinet – china plates, cut-glass salad bowls, matched sets of glasses, and so on. In the crystal cabinet in my home back in Eildon, my father kept more than crockery and glassware items. He was once given a second-hand electric shaver, and it went straight into the crystal cabinet, together with a fountain pen, a Ronson lighter and a pair of leather gloves. These items were not only 'too good' for regular use; they were too good for any use at all, and were taken out only to allow special visitors (my grandparents, for example) to briefly handle them.

Happiness was the elusive thing. I had been a very happy little kid, up to a certain age. The components of that happiness were probably no more remarkable than those of other lives, but the sum overwhelmed me. Trapped in the memory of my senses were fumes, images, sounds and tastes that would jolt me into a trance when sunlight found a certain path through clouds, when shadows of a certain density moved on a ceiling, when the barking of a dog carried over a certain distance on an otherwise soundless afternoon. I wanted Eden again. The cricket bat and the typewriter could provide only brief holidays from desperation.

I saved money. When I had twenty pounds, I went to a travel agency and asked about fares to the Seychelles. It was not possible to travel from Australia directly to the Seychelles, as it turned out. What you might do was travel to Ceylon, catch a boat to Mombasa, then another to the Seychelles. The fare to Ceylon was seventy pounds, one way. I paid a deposit on the boat fare, allowing myself four months to save the balance. My plan was to show my stories to the editor of a big newspaper in Ceylon, get a job as a reporter or book reviewer, save more money, then head off to Mombasa and finally to the Seychelles. In preparation, I sold my cricket bat and bought a beach towel.

Ship

MY FATHER WAS reluctant to let me, at sixteen, sail off to Ceylon. At the same time, he was impressed by my initiative. 'Wouldn't of believed he had it in him,' he said to me. (He'd formed a habit of talking to me in this indirect way when he was offering praise.) 'Nope, wouldn't of believed it.' What he did believe was that I had a return ticket and some hundreds of pounds in my pocket. That's what I'd told him. He also believed that I had guaranteed employment in Ceylon. I believed it, too, in a way. I was surprised myself when I was later forced to admit that I had no return ticket, no guaranteed employment, and only two pounds in my pocket.

The folly of my plan didn't properly hit home until I turned a corner down at the pier and saw the ship. It was a huge white thing, terrifying. The portholes somehow made it grin. I wanted to run away. 'Greek ship, is it?' my father said. He'd come to see me off. He insisted on carrying my suitcase. 'Don't speak Greek, do you?' My father's suspicion of my reading extended to the belief that I may have picked up foreign languages on the sly. 'Listen, I'm not coming on board,' he said. He handed me my suitcase and sniffed, and walked away for a moment to wipe his eyes. 'One thing,' he said. 'You know we love you. I'm y' dad, wherever you are. You get in trouble, I want to know, okay?' He walked away to wipe his eyes again. 'Shouldn't be letting you do this, should I?' he said. He walked away again, but this time didn't turn back.

In my cabin, I dressed myself carefully in my new green suit. The green suit was the closest I could come to the sort of attire that more sophisticated people wore. In trying to approximate the figure that an expensively dressed gentleman would cut, I had under estimated the importance of physique. My green suit gave me the appearance of a tall, thin grasshopper. The trousers were tight and too short, and showed too much of my white tennis socks. The jacket, quilted and with gold buttons impressed with the image of a Roman emperor, fitted me a little too loosely. Lacking a waistcoat, I wore a green cardigan, unaware that the plaited leather buttons of the cardigan diminished the impact of the daring, imperial buttons of the jacket. My shoes were stylishly pointed. I thought I looked smart, rakish, dangerous and cosmopolitan. My confidence was reinforced by the coolly appraising looks of the other passengers as I made my way to the dining salon for the first dinner out of port.

I began to imagine myself coping. As I took my seat at the table, I experienced one of those warm updrafts of conviction. But these thermals can falter in seconds. The Greek woman beside me asked quietly if I wouldn't prefer to sit with my mama and papa. I didn't understand for a minute or so. 'You going – by yourself?' she exclaimed, and when I confirmed this, she whispered to her husband. He studied me sceptically, then shrugged.

It was a struggle to hold on to the sophisticated image. But I had fifty pounds that my father had given me for postage stamps – he wanted no excuses about staying in contact. I went up to the bar on the open deck and ordered a dry martini – my first. Drinks were cheap on the open seas. I ordered a second and a third, impressed with the taste. I had never seen an olive before. I strolled back to my cabin (shared with five other passengers), carefully hung up my green suit, placed the three olives in the drawer of my bedside table and went to sleep.

I woke in terror. I looked at my watch and saw that I'd slept for fifteen hours. The cabin was empty. The rackety, smiling Greeks in the other five bunks must have gone up on deck. The motion of the ship was an ugly swagger. I had gone away from everyone who knew or cared about me.

I lifted my suitcase onto my bunk and opened it. On top was my typewriter, my little Olivetti. Next came my books, thirty of them. I stacked them beside the bunk, reassured by their familiarity. I put the typewriter under the blanket, then climbed in myself, clutching *Doctor No* and *The Sun Also Rises* to my chest. I began to feel better. I fingered the typewriter keys and thought of the novel I might write that combined the best of Ian Fleming and Hemingway. Then I dressed in my green suit and went up on deck for some more dry martinis.

Loneliness, I discovered, is dense. One layer builds on another, packing it down. I lay in my cabin all day, reading, fretting, yearning. The Greek lady at the dining table had taken to cutting my meat into small pieces and exhorting me to leave a clean plate. She would croon softly, 'Too thin, too thin...' I had fallen in love with her, but also with a dozen other women. I wished just one of them would come to my cabin and allow me to speak to her wittily about literature before I took off her clothes and she smothered me with her breasts. I composed love letters to the Greek lady, telling her of my admiration for Greek civilisation and Plato and so on.

I roamed the corridors late at night, hoping that a door would open and one of the many carefree girls I saw on deck during the day would wrench me inside and force me onto the cabin floor. I became a witness to the post-midnight life of the passengers. Alone in the deck lounge, a chubby girl with a mass of tight red curls like a russet cauliflour practised the lines of the argument she intended to have with her boyfriend. A shirtless old man played cards by himself on the floor of a C deck corridor. One of the carefree girls I so coveted slipped into the shadowed alcove in which I was suffering, bent nimbly and removed her pants from under her dress, then disappeared. An Englishwoman carried her son out onto the games deck, one hand muffling his mouth; she belted the hell out of him, then carried him back below, her hand again over his mouth.

Most arresting of all was a woman in a nightie standing at the rail on the stern, nursing the tiniest of babies. The woman's face in the moonlight was a green mask of fatigue and despair. I thought she was going to throw the baby overboard, but as I inched closer I heard the murmur of her song: '… little star, how I wonder what you…' I had to admit to disappointment. If she had tossed the baby into the wake, I would have dived in and saved it. I would have denied hero status when interviewed for the ship's newspaper: "'I just happened to be there at the time," passenger Hillman insisted.'

I could feel my brain – against my will – working out the details of another magnificent display of daring, like the Myers façade. Loneliness becomes looniness, after a bit. Whether madness is murderous or farcical is just a matter of temperament. Denied a good motive for jumping into the sea by that tired mum, I thought I might jump in for no reason at all. I was a good swimmer. I could imagine staying afloat for a very, very long time in the warm Indian Ocean. Eventually, I would bob ashore on the African coast, which didn't look all that far away on the map near the Purser's office. And so I began to plan this epic freestyle crossing of the Indian Ocean – I would need to take some oranges, and my sheath knife to fend off sharks. I had a very good sheath knife. I had packed it in case I needed a subsidiary source of income once I reached the Seychelles. My primary source would be writing tales for magazines, but during periods of writer's block I would dive for pearls and giant clams in the reefs. I had also brought two packs of playing cards with me. I could make a living as a gambler if all else failed.

The big obstacle to the Indian Ocean swim was my typewriter. My books were a problem, too. How could I lug them along with me? Eventually, I worked something out. If I were to partially blow up three or four balloons (balloons were no problem, they were everywhere in the entertainment lounge) and stuff them into my suitcase, then seal the suitcase with tape, the thing would float, and I could push it ahead of me. I found the balloons and tucked them into the case, but it made a very heavy sea chest, I had to admit. I fretted over the problem for days, then put it aside and threw myself into preparing a costume for the fancy dress party in the entertainment lounge. I would go as an Arab – or not as an Arab, but as T. E. Lawrence. I was crazy about T. E. Lawrence. I'd seen the movie. When Peter O'Toole strode along the roof of the wrecked train in his flowing white fairy-tale robes, I flipped.

I felt sublime on the night of the fancy dress party. I'd tossed down four or five dry martinis while stalking about the deck in my Lawrence outfit. The outfit was made from bed sheets. My sheath knife hung from my belt. My pointed shoes were not in keeping with the robes, but I'd tied some coloured streamers to the laces to give the footwear a festive look. By the time of the fancy dress parade, I was floating.

I hit the floor with the other contestants, circling again and again past the judges. It occurred to me that I needed some sort of flourish to properly attract their attention. I drew my knife from its sheath and held it aloft, just as Lawrence might have done. I was pounced on immediately by a couple of ship's officers, who wrestled me into a corridor and confiscated the knife. One of them thrust his nose against mine and dilated his nostrils like a foxhound. 'Too much beers!' he hissed. 'Where your father?' I refused to answer. My feelings were hurt. The two officers let me go, but only after a lot of scowling. I was told that I could retrieve my knife from the Purser in the morning.

Up on deck, wounded, bitter, I gazed at the silver wash coiling against the hull. Not so far away in the black night lay the coast of Africa. I climbed the railing with some difficulty, hampered by my robes. When I leapt, I made slow progress.

The same officers were now holding fast to my robes. I was made to sit in a deckchair and listen to a stern lecture, a tag-team lecture, with one officer taking over from the other at regular intervals. The first officer spoke about the terrible things that alcohol could do to a person. The second spoke about death by drowning. The first dismissed the luxury of drowning and promised me that I would first be mangled in the ship's screw. The second asked if I had any brains in my head. In the end, they let me go.

After the swimming-to-Africa debacle, self-preservation prevailed once more. I stopped drinking. I enjoyed periods of reflection. I wandered the ship without paying too much attention to anything. I decided I would live an essentially solitary life, and probably work for world peace. During one of these melancholy saunters, I discovered the ship's library. It was a beautifully made room with dark wooden panelling. It was deserted when I found it and deserted every time I visited it. Amongst the books (in tall shelves that had been carpentered to fit around portholes) I came across writers who were new to me (well, a lot of writers were new to me) and entered into a reading rhapsody. I took *Pale Fire* down from the shelves, read the foreword and the 999-line poem where I stood, reached for *Soldier's Pay* and read well into that, then harvested a further half-dozen volumes of whatever caught my attention and retired to the librarian's desk. (The librarian, so far as I could ever judge, did not exist.) It was bliss. A hum developed in my head and heart that harmonised perfectly with the burr of the ship's engines. I lived between the library, the dining room and my cabin for a week.

I don't know quite what it is that we might learn from reading, other than the template of narrative. My reading didn't enhance my ability to cope with life. It didn't place my fantasies in relief, so that I could see them for what they were. On the contrary. *For Whom the Bell Tolls* convinced me that my destiny lay in blowing up bridges on which fascists were advancing. Faulkner's *Soldier's Pay* gave me the feeling that war was probably very exciting, so long as you didn't get shot too often. *Brideshead Revisited* nudged me in the direction of a career at Oxford, perhaps after the war on fascists. *Doctor Zhivago* made me a more convinced communist. Perhaps the reader can learn from literature only what he or she already knows – perhaps it's confirmative rather than educative. I knew nothing.

The ship, meanwhile, was drawing closer to Ceylon. Passengers intending to disembark at Colombo were invited to gather with their cabin luggage outside the Purser's office. I lugged my suitcase down, filled in a form for the Ceylonese immigration officers, then spent an hour on the deck rail gazing in anxious rapture at the great green bay, at the dirty yellow sky above the ramshackle city, at the hundred small boats muddling toward us on the wrinkles of the sea. Men as black as shoes screamed at the passengers, hoisting up wares in nets on the end of long poles – cowries, conches, tennis shoes, yellow plaster buddhas. Bolts of cloth were unfurled, one after another, the merchants keening with nonchalant hysteria for attention. I noticed that many were no more than boys. The only difference between the boys and the full-grown men was age. All did the same work; all wore expressions of cheerful disdain. *'Give us your money then go to hell.'* They terrified me, the merchants, but I was attracted, too. They were tough, lean, nimble. If I could survive in the city that was home to these pirates, I could survive anywhere.

I picked out a three-storey colonial building down near the dock. That might be the headquarters of the newspaper I would work for – the *Colombo Herald*, the *Ceylon Mercury*, whatever it would turn out to be called. I saw myself setting off for work with a notebook and a couple of biros, interviewing conch hustlers down at the dock. Friendships would develop. I would become a familiar figure around Colombo, hailed by the mighty and the humble alike. Later, I'd head up into old India, and do for the Indians what I'd done for the Ceylonese. I'd be firm but affectionate with the women I came to know.

But the Ceylonese immigration officers stuck a spoke in my wheel. I was called up by the Purser and asked to sit at a folding card-table with two men who looked like the boat merchants but wore white shirts and a weary manner.

'What brings you to Ceylon, Mister Hillman?'

'Just having a look.'

'What is your profession?'

'Reporter.'

'Reporter?'

'For newspapers.'

'I see. Well, Mister Hillman, according to your form, you have brought no money with you. Is that correct?'

'I've got some money.'

'I see. How much, would you say?'

'Seven pounds Australian. Seven pound ten Australian.'

'I see. And it says here you have no return ticket?'

'No.'

'How do you intend to buy things? Food?'

'I'll get a job.'

'A job?'

'On the newspaper.'

'I see. Mister Hillman, you cannot come to Ceylon. You must have money. You must have a ticket. You must have employment. Where are your parents?'

Highly insulted once more, I took my suitcase back to my cabin and sat moodily on my bunk, thinking bitterly of all the obstacles that ambition had to leap. Eventually, one of the ship's officers knocked at the door and invited himself in. He was fat and sour and could barely control his impatience. While he interviewed me, sitting on a bunk opposite, he held his hat in both hands and drummed one foot on the floor.

'Do you know what now?' he said. 'Now you come to Greece.'

'To Greece?' I began to warm to the idea instantly. But new plans would have to be made.

'Yes! Because you have no money! You have no ticket! You come to Greece and go to the Embassy Australia.'

'Oh.'

'You should be not on this ship! Where is your mama?'

'In Australia.'

'Ha! You go home, your father and mama smack you on the backside!'

'Why?'

'Why! Why! Because you *have no money*! We take you to Greece, you go back to Australia!'

I thought this plan absurd, but I didn't say so.

The officer glared at me for a little longer, then shook his head in disgust and left. He took my passport with him.

If that's the way it is, I thought, then that's the way it is. I went up to the deck bar for a couple of dry martinis, then to the library. Hmm. *Madame Bovary*. I'd heard of it. I took it back to my cabin and started reading.

The five Greeks in my cabin began to take a real interest in me after the ship left Colombo. I explained why I was still on board, and they listened with respect. Then they laughed and slapped their thighs and punched me on the shoulder. They thought I'd pulled a swifty. They winked and pointed at their temples. One of them, a boy of about eighteen with the shoulder span of a sixteen-wheel highway clipper, offered to introduce me to the girlfriend of his girlfriend when we reached Piraeus. 'More beautiful,' he said. 'More good for you.'

Madame Bovary thrilled me, but it troubled me, too. I thought, whoa, I'm not like Emma, am I? Always thinking there should be something more? A complainer? Mere discontent was treated with scorn by my father. He would be sympathetic if there was an identifiable cause – 'I'm afraid of the dark' – but if I complained of just feeling miserable, he'd fly into a rage. 'People don't feel crook for just *nothing*! If you feel crook, what's wrong with you? You're not a *girl*, are you? Jesus Christ, look at Benny Fenshaw! Five kids to feed and he's told he hasn't got a job any more! His bloody missus nagging him to death. How do you think *he* feels? You've got a bloody roof over your head. You've got your three meals a day. You've got your bloody family. What the hell *more* do you want?'

This was working-class stoicism with a little poison added (the man–woman relationships of the working class in my father's generation were often conducted on the frontier of homicide), but it was also the moral truth and seemed inarguable to me. Even today, as an approximate adult, my standard rejoinder to bleak voices from within comes straight from my father's phrase-book of moral correctives: 'Jesus, it's not the friggin' Burma–Siam railway, is it?'

Persisting with Flaubert, I started on *Sentimental Education*, but it was over my head. I took out a couple of William books instead, and enjoyed them as much as anything I'd ever read. Whatever I opened, I imagined myself getting to know the author, usually delighting him or her with my conversation. It wasn't only writers that I believed would welcome me into their homes and hearts. I also made myself the great friend and advisor to pop stars. Back in Eildon I would cast a spinner into the waters of the lake and, while I reeled it slowly back in, contemplate the sort of buddy I would make for Bob Dylan if he should come wandering down the shoreline. I wouldn't gush, and Bob would appreciate that. He would have had his fill of fans and lackeys. No, I wouldn't even acknowledge that I knew who he was, at first. 'So, how are they biting?' Bob might ask. 'Oh, so so,' I'd answer.

But if I was to survive, I had to make plans of a plain and practical sort. I was dim, but I was not without some of the normal and useful resources of other people. I decided to save some of my remaining money for Greece. My remaining money amounted to seven pounds. Okay, so that's five pounds for dry martinis for the rest of the voyage and two pounds to help me along when I left the ship. Braced by this new commitment to sense and responsibility, I relaxed completely. In the lovely library, I sipped the martinis and read my way steadily into the Suez Canal.

I didn't know we were in the Suez Canal until I wandered hazily up on deck and found myself staring at Egypt, at the fawn sand, at date palms, at camels. I was flabbergasted. Lightheaded on gin and vermouth, the added delight of Suez produced one of those episodes of happiness so finely wrought that you become a work of art. Everyone enjoys maybe a half-dozen such experiences in a lifetime. At any other time you endure the collapsing possibility of ever knowing that woman standing only the length of your shadow away with arms bare to the shoulders. But at those moments when you become art, you *narrate* the next few moments of your life.

Or not. Because there was, in fact, a woman with arms bare to the shoulders standing close by as I gazed at Egypt. She glanced at me; I glanced at her. She was beautiful. She wore a skirt that the breeze lifted softly.

'Isn't it wonderful,' she said, speaking of the sand and the date palms and camels.

'Wonderful,' I agreed.

'You feel you'd like to run barefoot to Cairo, don't you?'

'Yep.'

She moved closer to me, and without another word, put her arm around my shoulders and squeezed. She was, I suppose, a little over twenty. The honey-beige colour of her skin seemed more a product of ripening than of tanning.

'I don't know whether I should say this, but I wanted to tell you something. You drink a bit too much.'

'Pardon?'

'It's not my business, I know, but I do think you drink too much. I see you up here quite a lot. You nearly always have a drink in your hand.'

'Oh.'

'You're a nice boy. You shouldn't spoil yourself. Do your mum and dad know you come up here drinking? I won't tell them. I just wondered.'

Back in my cabin, I fought back tears. If a messenger from heaven had offered me fifteen minutes of being kissed and fondled by the woman with the bare arms, and my throat cut in the sixteenth minute, I would have accepted the deal without a second's hesitation.

On the morning of the ship's arrival at Piraeus, all the Greeks wept. They threw their hands towards the sky, shook their heads, dashed the tears from their cheeks. The boy who'd offered me his girlfriend's girlfriend (and I had not forgotten about that) grabbed me by my waist and lifted me off the deck. 'Ellas!' he cried. 'Ho boy!'

The Purser called me to his office and returned my passport. He produced a tatty map of Athens and described the route I should take to the Australian Consulate. 'They will look after you,' he said. 'We have informed them. They talk to your mummy and father. Two weeks, back you go to Australia. Okay? You understand?'

'Sure,' I said.

IT IS WINTER and I am nine years old. I am at work on a terraced slope in the Cathedral Ranges, digging small holes in the earth and spreading black topsoil evenly around each hole. The holes are dug in a contoured line following the undulations of the mountain and spaced at intervals of four yards. Fifty other people, men and boys, are at work in the same way. Each has a line to follow.

A further fifty people, all adults, shuffle along the line of small holes and plant a tiny pine sapling in each excavation. Then the planters push the black soil in around the sapling and pat it flat with their hands. If you pause from your work for a minute, you can hear from all over the mountain the dull tom-toms of men flattening the black soil.

The ranges have a modelled shape. From a certain vantage point, they look like a cathedral. But this depends. You might see the shape as a great ship, an ocean liner, the bow pushing west into the turbulent grey clouds and the bridge rearing behind. Or as a walled fortress erected to guard the bounty of the even taller mountains beyond.

This is my first formal employment. I will be paid four pounds for the day's work. I feel enormously privileged to be employed. The happiness inside me jingles like a tambourine. There's nothing I would not do to prove myself as a worker on this plantation project. If the foreman, Gary Yates, a friend of my father's, asked me to work barefoot in my undies, I would, despite the cruel, blue winter wind that bullies its way down the slopes, pushing my hair to one side. My father is watching me. He's working three rows above me. It is of the greatest importance to me that the planter of my row doesn't catch up with me. That's the test – to stay ahead of the planter. If the planter catches you, you're done for.

I am still ahead of the planter at lunchtime, and pleased about it. I sit with my father to eat my sandwiches. My hands and bare legs are painfully cold, but I am unconcerned. My father sits with his elbows resting on his knees. He has finished his sandwiches and is now holding a mug of tea from a thermos and dragging on a cigarette, an unfiltered Temple Bar. He sniffs twice and then hunches his head into his shoulders a little. It's a way he has of preparing himself when he has something important to say.

'Miss your family?' he asks.

'No,' I say, shocked.

'What, you don't miss your family?'

'Nope.'

I'm already on fire with embarrassment. My father never mentions my mother to me. I only ever hear of her when one of his mates brings her up. That hasn't happened for a couple of years now. I don't want my father to talk about her any more. I am wrenched about by shame and fear. My happiness of a little while ago is smashed to pieces.

'I think you do,' my father says after a minute or so. 'I think you miss your family.'

I wait for the blow.

'Boy your age needs a mum,' he says – and there it is, like being thumped in the stomach and left sick.

'And Bobby, listen old pal, I need a family, too. Okay? Mightn't look like it, but a grown-up bloke can get good and proper sick of things. Y' know?'

He pauses again. Waiting, my prayer is Make him stop.

My father sniffs twice. He is happy. I can see that.

'Now, you won't remember your mum much, I suppose...'

I know that what I am about to do will seem mad, but I have to do it. I run away. I run down the hill to the muddy clay road where the six trucks that brought all of us to the mountain are waiting. I sit on the ground beside the trucks and stay there the whole afternoon. My father can probably see where I am from up on the mountain. He leaves me be. Throughout the afternoon, my distress lapses and returns. The huge bowl of the valley brims with angry cloud. Rain falls briefly, then flies off over the summit of the mountain.

The evening dark has begun to settle by the time the workers come down from the mountain. As the boys pass me, they roll their eyes or snort in disgust or simply glance with curiosity. The men don't look at me at all. My father kneels down in front of me and takes my ears in his fingers and wiggles them. He doesn't hold it against me that I am insane.

A week later, a woman I have never seen before moves into our house on Ninth Street with her three children. I could not be more surprised if a tribe of Zulus in full battle dress had appeared in the kitchen.

My father introduces me. He calls the blond woman 'Gwen'. The children are Jenny, Sharon and little Jeffrey. I shake hands and smile as if I understand something that I don't understand at all.

I call the blond woman 'Gwen' for the rest of the day. Her expression is odd whenever I talk to her. That night, my father takes me down to the woodshed and lights the Tilley lamp. He produces a sixpence and asks me to put out my hand.

'This is for you,' he says. 'I want you to call Gwen 'Mum' from now on. Will you call her 'Mum'?'

'Nope.'

'You'll make your dad very, very happy if you call her 'Mum'. Will you call her 'Mum' from now on?'

'Okay.'

When we return to the house, I go to the kitchen where Gwen is stirring a cauldron of pea and ham soup.

'Hello, Mum,' I say, as awkwardly as you would expect.

Gwen looks at me and lifts her chin, and her lips curl satirically.

'Uh huh,' she says. She knows what has gone on.

'What is it?' she says, not quite letting me off the hook.

'Nothing,' I say. I leave the kitchen and head back down to the woodshed, and sit there in the dark for half an hour, sick with shame.

 Highway

MY SUITCASE WAS packed. I'd had my green suit pressed by the cabin steward. I walked down the gang-plank and kept walking. The town was old and ramshackle, and almost everyone I saw looked vaguely demoralised. The air was full of the noxious fumes of the disorderly traffic. The Purser, acting on orders or from the goodness of his heart, had given me a handful of drachma notes – the first foreign money I'd ever seen. It seemed a lot to me. I had no intention of following the route to the Australian Consulate, and was instead intending to hitch my way to Germany. I'd earn a lot of money there, then head off to the Seychelles.

I thought it might be wise to buy a packet of biscuits and a bottle of Coke for the long road ahead. In a roughly cobbled street I stepped into a gloomy shop, which turned out not to be a shop but a bar. A number of women in short skirts and tight tops were sprawled on chairs, looking ill with boredom. I put down my suitcase, smiled in what I hoped was a winning way and asked the barman, who seemed as bored as the women, for a bottle of Coke to take away. I was not so stupid as to ask for a packet of biscuits. The barman placed an opened bottle of what was surely beer in front of me. I offered the handful of drachma notes and the barman took all but one. The oldest and least attractive of the bored women put her hip against my groin and lifted one of her breasts out of her blouse for a moment. She wobbled her tongue between her lips, then asked me something I didn't understand. Another woman, more attractive than the first, roused herself from her chair, took my hand and tugged me upstairs to a small room with lace curtains and a hand basin in the corner. I took my suitcase with me.

What I was thinking was this: perhaps I should put in some practice here in order to prepare myself for the more desirable women of the Seychelles. It was not destined to work out, however, because the woman wanted money. I showed her what I had – my two-pound note and my only remaining drachma note – and she lost all interest. I stood silently beside her while she went to sleep on a rickety chaise longue. A *Monopoly* board was open on the bed. Little wooden houses and hotels were set up on most of the properties. I apologised to the woman's sleeping form, picked up my suitcase and left.

I was a competent hitch-hiker; back home, I'd hitched all the time. I realised I was an easy person to pick up, for nothing about me looked menacing. Quite the contrary. I'd also realised that it was pointless to walk while hitching. If you were walking, drivers could persuade themselves that it was within your power to reach your destination on foot. Also, it was difficult for drivers to get a look at your unthreatening face and form if your back was to them. I stood erect on the roadside with my face to the oncoming traffic, attempting to look polite and also pitiable.

One ride and another and another took me from Piraeus to Athens (which looked as if it had been built, badly, about two hours before my arrival) and through Athens to a leafy suburb of big, attractive houses surrounded by tall walls. Left standing on the roadside in this silent and pleasant suburb, I thought I would read for a while. Before long, a Mercedes rolled gracefully out of a nearby driveway. The driver, a flawlessly groomed woman in white, asked if I was a student. I thought it best to say that I was. She asked me where I would like to go. I said, to Germany.

Cruising along towards somewhere, the woman asked a long series of questions about conditions for students in various European countries. I answered all of her questions. Suddenly, the woman brought the car to a halt and put one hand over her face. She was weeping. I thought she must have fallen in love with me. Her weeping made hardly any sound at all. After a few minutes, she shook off her tears, looked straight ahead and told me I would have to get out of the car. I asked if there were anything I could do. She laughed mirthlessly and patted my cheek. 'When you grow up, be a good boy, you understand? Be a good boy.' No sooner had I closed the boot after retrieving my suitcase than the Mercedes ground out a furious U-turn and sped off.

I puzzled over the woman's behaviour as I waited for my next lift. I could only make sense of it by thinking of the woman as Chekhovian. She had probably just lost a large estate. Possibly she was married to some decrepit old idiot and was dying of unfulfilment. When she saw me on the side of the road, reading my book, she maybe thought she could begin a new life with me in Germany, but then realised that we would have to live on next to nothing and didn't have the strength of character to give up her pampered existence for the sake of love, no matter how much she wanted to. As I fashioned the story that I thought I might write about the woman, I found myself thrilled with the line, 'The tears she shed as she farewelled the young man were as bitter as olives.' I knew about olives, having eventually nibbled on one only, from a shipboard dry martini. The woman I would write of was more beautiful and thirty years younger, and naked from the waist up.

Further rides north took me through the dreary cities of Lamia and Larisa. It had been dark for some hours when I was dropped off in the middle of nowhere by a furiously bickering carload of Bulgarians. They were heading for Sofia, not for Germany. I sat on my suitcase, staring futilely into the dark for some indication of the direction I should now take. It was late November, almost winter, and the night was cold.

I had to give up on waiting in one place for a lift. The highway was deserted of traffic of any sort. I headed down the road towards nothing with tears as bitter as olives welling in my eyes. I wished I were home and still working in Bertie's and had some food and money. I was terribly tired and Greece seemed such a barren place, no trees, no paddocks, the cities a mess. And my suitcase could not have been heavier if it had been full of house bricks. A terrible fear was curdling into panic. I feared that I might be completely mad, and that everybody knew except me. The Chekhovian woman in the car – she might have noticed it. Maybe that was why she had suddenly abandoned me. But as I trudged on, I decided that I would refuse to believe that I was mad. Even if it were true, it would be better not to believe it. Sometime in the future, when I was warm and secure, I would examine my behaviour and come to some balanced assessment of my sanity.

After a lot of walking I saw a roadhouse standing forlorn in the silence of the night, as if abandoned there. It was an unadorned roadhouse – it didn't seem to take itself seriously. I trudged inside, barely able to keep my suitcase from dragging.

Two men were playing cards at a formica-topped table and, behind a glass-fronted refrigerated cabinet, a woman was guarding the only fare on display – a single doughnut. The card players looked up briefly from the table; the woman paid no attention to me at all. I negotiated the purchase of the doughnut with my last drachma note, then headed back out into the night.

Further along the road, I made out a few dim lights that suggested a camp rather than a township. I came to a tiny shack, a kiosk, with a young man and two older men sitting outside on canvas stools. By this time, I was crying. The two older men looked both surprised and a bit offended – offended perhaps by my sookiness and my appearance. I blubbered out that I had no home, no money, no food, no nothing – in effect, throwing myself on their mercy. The two older men bestirred themselves slowly from their stools and held a candle to my face, chatting back and forth. One threw his arm around my shoulders, the other made small clucking sounds of sympathy. The young man, who seemed to be the proprietor of the kiosk – pistachios and pumpkin seeds were all it offered – put two hands to the side of his head and made the universal sleepy-time gesture. He gathered the three canvas stools, locked up the kiosk and signalled for me to follow him.

As we approached his home, he whistled twice. A girl opened the door for us, greeting me shyly after listening to an explanation from the young man. He made me understand, by pointing to the ring on his finger and the ring on the woman's finger, that they were married. Within, the house was furnished in the simplest way, nothing but the necessities. Out of the darkness an old woman appeared, made the sign of the cross, then vanished. The young man and I sat in silence at the kitchen table, he opening and closing his hands and shrugging to cover the awkwardness, me smiling in the most ingratiating way I could summon.

I didn't know what was being offered, but probably a place to sleep for the night, for the young woman was busy with blankets and sheets. The young man would want money, I thought, and wretchedly, fearing the cold and dark outside, I made him understand that I had no money, could not pay. He threw up his hands, making, so it seemed, embarrassed denials, then laughing as he explained it to his wife. She came at last and sat with us at the table, smiling and pretty, her dark hair tied at the back of her head. After more awkward smiles and embarrassed laughter, the young man showed me to the makeshift bed that had been set up on the floor beside an old iron double bed on the far side of the kitchen. Beneath the sheets and blankets, I gloried in the relief of rest for a time, but then felt ashamed. My loneliness and neediness had brought me all the way across the world to cadge hospitality from people who could not afford such luxuries as loneliness.

Some time after I'd snuggled down, the young man and his wife came to bed. I listened to their whispers, and to the progress of the whispers into murmurs and soft laughter, then into love-making, to his rapid endearments (as I supposed) and her moans and gasps. Afterwards, they spoke quietly with each other for a long time. I think they went to sleep before I did.

The couple gave me breakfast in the morning, and the young woman wrapped a sandwich in brown paper and handed it to me as I departed. The husband took me down to the road and told me where to wait for a ride. He took himself off with a wave, but then hurried back. He put a finger under each of my eyes and screwed his face up into an imitation of sobbing. Then he waved his finger under my nose and smiled. 'Don't be a baby any more,' was surely the message.

I was chastened for a while. But in the lulls of the day, waiting for rides, I thought back to the small, bare house and the lovely young wife, and it came over me that happiness was to be found in just such a place with just such a wife. My pretty young wife's name would be Athena, but she would look very much like the young wife who had given me the sandwich I was carrying in my pocket. We would live on a farm in some more attractive part of Greece than any I'd so far laid eyes on – somewhere green and vivid, where peasants spent the whole day singing and dancing and drinking wine. Being a peasant girl, Athena would naturally want babies. We would have a number of babies, but only after maybe five years of incessant love-making. Athena would be somewhat in awe of my erudition, and indeed the entire peasant community would think of me as a genius, and bring their troubles to me to solve. I would be supported in my writing and study by a subscription taken up by the cheerful peasants. They would jokingly, but warmly, speak of me as 'the scholar', and take pride in showing me off to neighbouring communities. I would probably have a number of love affairs with other maidens of the village, but Athena would be very understanding.

These reveries lasted for the whole day and into the night, by which time I had been delivered, after a number of lifts, to Polykastro, a tiny village in Macedonia. It was snowing in Polykastro when I arrived, and there were no lights to be seen. It was not long before I was blubbering again, and was rescued this time by a small posse of kids who gathered about me with grave looks, then hustled me off to a house where I was greeted by an entire family as if expected at just this time on just this day. It was the home, once again, of a poor family; mum, dad and two kids were all sitting by an open fire when I was ushered in. Whatever account of my sudden arrival was being given by the posse seemed unimportant to the dad. He waved the kids away, shook my hand and introduced me to the mum, to the son, to the daughter. I tried to smile, but the open fire so attracted me that I could barely concentrate. Like a dog that has slunk in from the cold, my eyes kept sliding toward the flames, and the pleading look in my eyes finally won me a spot by the hearth.

The mum served me a plate of something dominated by eggs and spinach, so delicious that I began to sniffle once more, but with gratitude. The daughter brought me a school atlas, and I pointed out my country and city. A whoop of delight came from the dad, and a big congratulatory slap on the back, as if he'd just learned that I'd swum from Australia to Greece then jogged overland to his front door. I was made to understand that one member of the family was absent – an elder son, by the sound of it, who was in Germany. I was put to bed in the absent son's room, which had been maintained to a particularly strict standard of housekeeping. I settled under crisp, white sheets, heaped blankets, slept like a baby and awoke to a hot breakfast.

An interpreter arrived a little after breakfast – a boy of about twelve whose uncle lived in Sydney. As he translated back and forth, he maintained that objective and disciplined air of the interpreter, smoothing out what seemed like surprise and alarm in the Greek he was taking in, and offering me a calmer English version.

'Where you going for this day?' he asked, prodded by the dad.

'To Germany.'

Sounds of surprise.

'Mister Kouriapoulis saying Germany many far.'

'Oh? Well, that's where I'm going.'

Shrugs, scratching of heads.

'Mister Kouriapoulis saying you too little – little? – too young for going to Germany.'

'I'll be right.'

Worried expressions.

'Mister Kouriapoulis saying you going to Germany on bus?'

'Hitch-hiking.' I displayed my thumb.

Sounds of alarm.

'Mister Kouriapoulis saying is bad.'

The upshot was that Mr Kouriapoulis paid my fare by bus to the border of Yugoslavia – a journey of an hour. He also produced four large, silver coins – Deutschmarks as it turned out, probably sent by his son – and made me understand (for the boy who had been translating had gone off to school, together with Mr Kouriapoulis' son and daughter) that these were for buying food (hand up to mouth, biting action, rubbing of tummy). I had earlier been given a piece of paper on which the boy who'd been translating had written Mr Kouriapoulis' name, his wife's name, and the names of the son and daughter. I was to write to Mr Kouriapoulis when I reached Germany and tell him that I was safe and in good employment. (I still have the piece of paper. It should be filed in a dossier under 'L' for Little Bastard, for I did not write to Mr Kouriapoulis.)

The bus to Yugoslavia stopped a little distance from the border. Together with thirty or so other passengers, I wandered towards a shack that was being guarded by a soldier dressed in what my reading of comic books prepared me to recognise as a Commie uniform; that is, an ill-tailored uniform with a lot of padding and big red stars pinned to it. The passengers were carrying light luggage, as if ready for a day trip, and not one of them seemed happy about the journey. I would later learn that they were Macedonians visiting other Macedonians across the border, but at the time I imagined them to be forced labour heading for work in dark cavities beneath the earth. Sure enough, they all climbed aboard a second bus after enduring the surly scrutiny of the soldier. As for me, it appeared that I would have to walk to wherever I was going. The soldier didn't think me worth serious attention.

The countryside was green and sweet, but here and there off the roadside and on the hillsides I noticed grim, bunker-like buildings that offended me with their ugliness. I was, in a cluttered part of my head where a host of ill-sorted beliefs lived a fairy-tale life, a dedicated communist. It seemed to me that my fellow communists could do a little more to please the eye, so far as architecture was concerned. In my imagination, communist states were full of glorious palaces and castles (now the homes of the workers), charming cottages and lots of other good old stuff. I expected the workers to be cheerful, spending a part of each day doing nothing much more than chuckling, and maybe singing. It was my further belief that communist women had very loose morals (a good thing) and put sex, particularly with visitors from non-communist states, high on their agendas (because by having sex with visitors, they were subverting capitalism – I think that was my reasoning.) So far (an hour into Yugoslavia), not so good. But perhaps I was in a bad-tempered corner of the country. Things would improve.

I was puzzling over the whole business when someone shouted from a distance away. I put my suitcase down and looked about. I was alone. The nearest building was a turret-shaped hut on a hillside a fair way off. I picked up my suitcase and resumed my journey. Again, the shout, a little louder. This time I saw a figure advancing downhill.

The figure became a soldier. He had a rifle, and the rifle was aimed at me. I was thrilled. As he drew closer, I could see that he was young, *very* young, in fact no older than me, surely. He approached me with a serious yet not uncompromising expression, as if the rules of a game were about to be discussed. Noticing my delight in having a genuine firearm aimed at me, he lowered the weapon and grinned. His teeth were not so good. 'Passaport!' he shrilled, and I smiled, fished out my passport and offered it to him. He propped his rifle against his flank while he studied my picture. The rifle fell to the ground and he left it there.

He handed back my passport (which bore no entry stamp, let alone a visa), grinned even more broadly and made a motion towards his mouth with two spread fingers. 'Cigarette!' he said. I raised my shoulders and displayed my empty hands – the international *alas!* gesture. He nodded, still grinning. 'Is Tray Ee?' he said, and I smiled and nodded. He put his hands together in front of his chest and gave a series of small jumps. 'Kang Crew!' he said. Then a very loud, very pissed-off shout from the turret put an end to this cultural exchange. The boy-soldier picked up his rifle, straightened his cap, and ran back up the hill. I was disappointed to see him go. I'd been hoping he'd let me hold his rifle for a little bit.

A series of rides in trucks built with a stern disdain for anything elaborate in the way of suspension took me to the city of Skopje. The city, even under a pale blue sky, had a grieved, wintery look. The people also seemed a bit sleety. Every glance was hedged with suspicion. The goodwill I'd met with in the north of Greece had encouraged me to believe that Europe had taken me to its heart, and I held it against the Yugoslavs that they weren't just a little more welcoming – me being a fellow communist.

That was one issue. Another was hunger. The day was getting on, and visions of the sort of food I would have loved to have seen laid out on a table began to torment me. Weetbix. Toast. Apricot jam. Sausages and mashed potatoes and gravy and tomato sauce. Tinned peaches. A big tub of Peters ice cream. I came to a bakery and drooled over the cakes in the window, spartan little pastries though they were. I went inside and displayed my silver coins. The woman behind the counter studied them aggressively, her jaw thrust out, and the customers in the shop joined in. Some senior person, probably the baker himself, was called in from the back. He shrugged laconically, and gave the thumbs up. Then I did something uncharacteristically sensible. I chose a fat loaf of bread instead of a bag full of cakes.

I had only the vaguest notion of the road I should take. Whenever a truck stopped for me I mentioned Germany, but if the driver indicated that he was going elsewhere, I changed my plans accordingly. This made for a lot of meandering. Sometimes I went through a town twice. Only trucks stopped. Yugoslavian car drivers never conceded the possibility of changing down a gear once they'd reached top. In any case, the truck drivers suited me fine. They were nearly all drunks, so I was able to rely on my experience of hitching with drunks back in Australia.

A drunk doesn't require much of you. You're offered a swig from a bottle (plum brandy in Yugoslavia, beer in Australia); you are invited to look at pictures of naked women in a magazine fetched from the glovebox, and to listen to tales of the drunk's legendary sexual exploits; a little later, you join in a song (back in Australia, 'The Green, Green Grass of Home', 'Do What You Do Do Well', 'From a Jack to a King'; the Yugo drunks were, I'm sure, singing local equivalents). The golden rule is this: sympathise. If the drunk is jolly, you're jolly; if the drunk becomes weepy, you go a fair way down that track with him. It all works out beautifully in the end.

But there was one local variation to the international rules of hitching with pisspots: the Yugo drunks wanted payment, and they weren't kidding. I didn't have any money except for my tatty Australian two-pound note, but I did have a suitcase full of items that the drunks could be persuaded to accept in lieu. My two packs of cards went first, then my pocket knife, followed by a couple of my copies of *Life* magazine, one of my four pairs of white socks and one of my spare ties (Paisley, much treasured). One drunk demanded my typewriter, but I said no, and I said it emphatically.

Night fell in what I think must have been Kosovo. My last ride had taken about two hours in a very low gear, climbing the mountains. We came to a branch road that looked as if it led exactly nowhere, and I got out with the sky turning a delicate quartz pink along the peaks. It seemed unlikely that I would get another ride that night, so I wandered into the scrub with my suitcase and unpacked two woolly blue blankets that I'd stolen from the ship. I put one on the ground and made myself a pillow out of my beach towel. I was feeling smug because I had in my suitcase the very items that would lend me comfort in this forsaken place: the loaf of bread and a candle. I actually had twelve candles. Back home when I was packing, it had suddenly struck me that I might want to write late into the night in my little hut in the Seychelles, and was it likely the Seychellois had electric light? It was not.

I fixed the candle in the ground, took off my tie and shoes and lay down with the second blanket pulled up to my chin. The bread was still fresh, still soft. I ate the entire loaf, watching the candlelight cast its own mini-sunset over the broad leaves above me. I was about to start reading *The Grapes of Wrath*, also stolen from the ship. I expected to enjoy it. The night was not cold, even so high up in the mountains, and in any case I was fully dressed in my green suit. Happiness filled my little world from horizon to horizon.

I awoke to birdsong of a sort I'd never heard before: a soft chattering that would suddenly rise to shrill argument, then abate again. I was surprised to find how far I'd gone into the forest and how alien its features were. I felt rested, and potent – ready to make terrific observations. A few years earlier I'd read in an obituary for Ernest Hemingway that he had so dedicated himself to capturing the real, the essential thing in landscape that he would set himself up somewhere out in the mulga with a notebook and pencil, just like a painter with easel and brushes. And he would get down what was real and essential just exactly as it unfolded. I wanted to do something of the sort.

I brushed off my green suit, put on my shoes and tie, then hunkered down with my typewriter on the grassy floor of the forest. I didn't quite know what I should observe, though. I typed out a few sentences about the trees. I recall noting that the trees were big and that the leaves of the trees were green and shiny.

Waiting on the side of the road for the first lift of the morning, I made an important decision. Come what may, I would not be a baby any more. Imagine Ernest Hemingway crying because he didn't have a place to sleep. Or imagine the scorn of Woody Guthrie if he had seen me sobbing because my feet were cold and my tummy empty. Nope, no more baby stuff. Also, it wouldn't be all that attractive to women, probably. I had once looked up a term I'd come across in a novel – *sang-froid* – and I was pretty sure that I wanted to be just that, or have that, or be known for that, or whatever it was that you did with it. *Sang-froid*.

But at the same time I was very hungry. I wished I'd kept some of the bread for brekky. As soon as I got to a decent-sized town, I would exchange my two-pound note and buy a pie and some chips and a bottle of Coke and a doughnut.

Hours passed. No trucks, no cars. Gazing at the mountain peaks, at the silent forest, at outcrops of bleak, grey stone, it occurred to me that I could possibly starve to death where I stood. What on earth would be the use of *sang-froid* if nobody could see me displaying it? The Zen book I'd read about the archer who tried too hard to hit the target had made the point that nothing much good can come of craving an audience, craving approval. But I couldn't see what else there was if you ruled out approval, applause. I might have been content to starve to death with great stoicism if only a thousand people had been watching. But to be found cold and still on the roadside without anyone knowing what I'd endured!

Looking back, I can see that it wasn't fame that I craved, but endorsement. I wanted people – anybody really – to shake their heads in disbelief and murmur, 'What a kid! What guts!' Back in my home town I once got a game in the local Juniors (the Thirds) footy team – I was hanging around when the captain was struggling desperately to find enough players. At half-time it was the habit of the coach of the senior team to stagger over, blind drunk from the nearby pub, and regardless of the score to counsel the players to show a bit of guts and determination: 'Y' fuckin' weak the pack of yez, fuckin' like a pack of fuckin' bridesmaids the way y' fuckin' tackle…' Then back he'd trot to the pub to put away a few more glasses before he led out the senior team. 'Guts and determination' was one of the immortal clichés of the code, and I loved the sound of it. I wanted with all my heart to be known for guts and determination.

Standing on that roadside in the mountains of Kosovo, I began to think of my death, and to compose the sort of obituary that I would have enjoyed reading: 'He left the comforts of home at the tender age of sixteen to try his luck in the wide world, but not in his wildest dreams could he have predicted that he would languish fatally in Yugoslavia and die a painful death from hunger and exposure. Yet not a murmur was heard from him as death stealthily approached across the frigid mountains. What his premature death robbed us of, it is too moving to dwell on, but in notes we find stories that rival those of Ernest Hemingway and Anton Chekhov at their best, full of extraordinary observations both of the landscape and of the many exceptional characters he came across in his strange travels...'

I was obliged to bed down in the Kosovo forest for a second night. This time, I was less jolly. My bread was gone. All I had were candles and books. I watched the sunset with my blanket at my chin. *The Grapes of Wrath* was providing no cheer. It is one thing to read of people struggling against the tide of the greatest economic calamity of the twentieth century when you feel happy and contented. It is quite another when you're hungry and cold. But I was at least able to dwell on the motives and incitements that had landed me on that mountain.

The fluctuations of thought, mimicking the flickering flame of the candle burning beside my cheek, eventually produced a bright moment of insight. This was not the first time I had set off in search of paradise, I realised. It was not the second, third or even tenth time. For years I had been fashioning Edens for myself. A lost city in the hills above my home town. A lost city in the valleys at the back of the green hills on the way to Thornton. A lost city on the island mountains across the lake. A lost city in the bush on Dry Creek Road. I carried sandwiches and cake and a tomato-sauce bottle full of cordial when I set off in search of those lost cities. And each time, the disappointment of not finding them was like a grievous and painful insult.

I wasn't expecting to find gold and jewels in these lost cities. I had no interest in gold and jewels. I was expecting radiance. Every surface would glow. The green of the grass would be more vivid than any green I had seen before. Creamy clouds would cross the blue sky in a silence so finely spun it would sound like music. The shadows of the clouds would follow the undulations of the hills and slide over wheatfields and forests. The trees would spread their branches so broadly that in the space beneath them whole families could live without any other shelter. The buildings were labyrinthine miracles, endless alleyways and tunnels lined with flowerbeds and banquet tables where you might pause to gobble down not two slices of toast and jam, but a hundred slices if you wished, and not only toast but crumpets, too, and not only one sort of breakfast cereal but a hundred sorts.

Surpassing the glowing colours of the city and the hills and the splendour of the architecture was the rich, warm, welcoming embrace of the people you met, the folk of the lost city. They smiled, and the beauty and warmth of their smiles blurred and melded, and you were left with an overwhelming feeling of sanction for anything you might say or display. Each feature of the lost city was airbrushed clean of scales or scabs. But more importantly, an airbrush had been expertly at work on the hearts and souls of these smiling people; what was mean or little or harsh or cruel had been smoothened, softened, made to disappear. The lost cities were made of a love that could not be exhausted, could not be altered; fall and tumble as you may, you were comforted.

As I lay there under my blue blanket, I did not go on to consider that these lost cities might be dramatised corollaries of longing, and even now I doubt that psychology could adequately explain them. I wanted paradise. The search was made more urgent by the furious hissing and scolding that my father and step-mother dished out to each other; by the faltering of joy in my life; by hard surfaces that bruised or sliced or left dark splinters under my skin. But even without these incitements to fantasy and escape, I would still have believed in lost cities. Where the idea of paradise came from, I don't know. Perhaps it was a sort of spiritual atavism. I believed the stories of Adam's children: stories of a secret garden to which we cannot return. I went peeking through holes in the wall of Eden, a desperado of happiness, mad to get inside, and always I was chased away, just as I'd been warned, by a killjoy character with a flaming sword.

Next day I was at last picked up by a surly truck driver who wanted payment immediately. Fees were usually settled at the end of the ride. I offered socks, my last pack of playing cards, and a novel (*Nicholas Nickleby*). The truck driver carried me for ten hours without speaking and without drinking anything at all. He kept a big, brown paper-bag of hard, mint lollies on the dashboard, and sucked his way through the lot. His cheeks flexed and the lollies clunked against his teeth. The names of towns and cities loomed in all their consonantal strangeness. Every time I saw a face in the street, its expression was sullen. The Yugoslavs seemed the most pissed-off people on earth. It was nightfall when the ride came to an end in Ljubljana, wherever that was.

Trudging through what appeared to be a suburb, I was forced to revisit the question of character. Approaching strangers with tears was no longer an option. How about approaching strangers to soberly request a place to sleep for the night? Anything wrong with that? I was working class, the Yugoslavs were working class. Brotherhood was the issue. Was it likely that Tom Joad would have felt squeamish about asking for a floor to sleep on? He was starving and cold; I was starving and cold. It was settled – I'd knock on doors and put my case. It does require a fair bit of egocentricity to draw a parallel between the experience of a boy on holiday without a cracker and that of a young man battling for survival in dustbowl America, but I was able to muster it. I was inflicting on the world the intolerable narcissism that most teenagers have the decency to reserve for their immediate families.

The suburbs of Ljubljana had not benefited from the cheerful, weekend attention that Australian suburbanites lavish on their plots. It was not that the lawns were left unmowed; there were no lawns, no gardens, no nature strips, no neat concrete curbing – just rows of stark, semi-detached bungalows. I went from door to door in the misty rain asking the dwellers if I might sleep on their floor. Looks of dismay and fear met me. Mothers shook their heads in panicky refusal, their puzzled children peeping out from behind them. Fathers stared at me in alarm, as if I were the harbinger of some new official torment. I'd been doorknocking for half an hour or so when a car screeched to a stop nearby and two policemen (by the look of them) demanded things that I could not understand. I was excited by this turn of events, just as I'd been by the young soldier a couple of days before. I had not the least fear that anything bad would befall me. Why should it? I wasn't doing anything wrong. And these guys had guns, always a fascinating sight to me.

Down at the station I was handed over to another policeman, a man with a great monument of a body and a magnificent, carved noggin. He looked like Omar Sharif twenty years on from Sherrif Ali, and twice the size. Every gesture he made underscored his vanity, but it was pleasant vanity. The mature, physically beautiful male (I've since noticed) is usually a very relaxed chap, often generous. This cop, Omar, gave me a few minutes to take in his magnificence, his perfect teeth, chemical blue eyes, the touches of central-casting grey at the temples, then quietly beckoned me to open my suitcase. He lifted out one item after another, chuckling all the while. The typewriter amused him especially. He held up the books at arm's length, and pretended to be reading in the manner of an egghead professor. I laughed, keen to ingratiate myself – a good policy.

When he came to my sheath knife, Omar could scarcely contain himself. He called in a subordinate and displayed the weapon, his blue eyes twinkling. He studied the knife with approval, then balanced its tip on the tip of a finger, moving his hand just slightly, expertly, keeping the knife upright. He suddenly spun the knife in the air. It landed dead on its point, quivering in the brown linoleum. I shook my head and whistled in unfeigned admiration. The weasel subordinate gave a grudging grimace and took himself off.

The *Life* magazines particularly pleased Omar. He flicked through an issue, turning the pages to me when a picture thrilled him. 'Chevrolet!' he said, and 'Bobby Kennedy!' and 'Elizabeth Taylor!' I told him to keep the magazine, and added a second. He protested, but agreed in the end. In return, he indicated that I would be brought some food, after my passport was scrutinised. He disappeared from my life with the two magazines, and a few hours later the weaselly constable brought me a quarter of an orange, a small piece of crumbly cheese and a glass of water. I sat under a portrait I recognised as that of President Tito, and read *The Grapes of Wrath*.

In the morning, an official arrived to review my case. While he was studying my passport, he munched on fresh toast fetched by the poor, exhausted weasel. Oh God, that toast! If only I'd been asked to confess to something with the promise of a slice of toast as a reward! When I returned to *The Grapes of Wrath*, my sympathy for the Okies on their journey to the Garden of Eden had passed all limits.

The upshot of my detention was that I was to be sent by train to Belgrade – a city which my maundering route across Yugoslavia had bypassed. I was horrified to discover, after consulting a map on the wall of the police station, that Ljubljana was no more than a skip and a jump away from Germany. The Yugos might have let me sneak over into Austria then on to Germany. But no, I was to present myself at the British Embassy in Belgrade, and the British, acting for the

Australian government, would send me back to Athens, and the Australian Consulate in Athens would send me back to Australia, and the whole journey would have been wasted. My duty was clear. I had to escape. But when I learned that I would be fed on the train, I decided that I would make my escape from Belgrade.

I was met at the station in Belgrade by an embassy car – a highly polished black Humber. The chauffeur looked familiar. I was sure he'd appeared in *From Russia With Love*, as a chauffeur. I risked asking him if any espionage went on in Belgrade. He didn't know what I was talking about. 'Spying,' I said. He shrugged. 'Who knows?' His answer satisfied me. A spy would always say, 'Who knows?' in reply to such a question.

Belgrade looked nothing like any other Yugoslavian city I'd passed through. It seemed prosperous and exuberant. If I were to run away here in Belgrade, I would likely find employment before long. I saw department stores. It was possible that I could get a job selling ladies' shoes and slippers. I had brought my reference from the Myer Emporium with me. It said, 'Robert showed diligence and left of his own accord.'

The British Embassy impressed me a great deal. It had a cobblestoned courtyard, where all the black, shining embassy vehicles parked. The door by which we entered the building was varnished and gleaming. The door knobs were polished brass. Within, the embassy looked exactly like the Oxford University of my imagining: varnished panels, tiled floors, and efficient men and women, perfectly groomed, calmly going about their business. I was shown into a room like a study, books in glass-fronted cases, an enormous desk on which a spotless white blotter was spread. A tall, urbane man in his forties smiled at me and flattered me terrifically by shaking my hand. His tailoring was impeccable.

Wandering about the embassy wide-eyed, I was sure that I detected admiration in the eyes of the people I met. It seemed to me that I was being checked out for possible employment – perhaps as a courier, conveying an important document or message to Athens. Or something grander. Maybe the embassy had been scouting for a clever boy with a bit of daring about him. I might be sent to London for training, then to Moscow. In London, I would perhaps be required to undergo torture to show that I could bear up. I might be wired to an electric shock machine, or have my head held under water. People would perhaps shout at me and abuse me, just to see if I had what it takes.

This was a mission that I'd been preparing myself for all my life. At the age of five I was convinced that I was being secretly watched by the army. The army wanted to see if I were good, thoughtful, considerate. Whenever I saw a tap left dripping anywhere about the town, I would turn it off firmly, then glance about with a stern expression to illustrate my disappointment with people who left taps dripping. I picked up pieces of litter, fragments of broken glass. If I found a dog wandering loose, I tried to find where it lived, or at least made sure it was off the road. None of this was done out of plain goodness (although I have remained a great worrier about stray dogs); it was done to impress the army. Every day I made sure that I looked up at the wall of the huge dam that loomed above the town, hoping that I would be the first to detect a crack in the wall, and that I would then be the first to give the alarm, and that I would be praised for saving the town, and a big tick entered beside my name in the dossier that was being kept on me by the army.

It was mid-afternoon when I arrived at the embassy – too late for me to be put aboard the train to Athens. I was placed in the care of a man who worked for the embassy in some capacity that seemed to cause him grief, for he spoke about it in a piqued manner, as if dwelling on it brought on dyspepsia. His name was Alex, and I was to stay with him for the night.

Alex drove me to his home in a down-at-heel suburb and cautioned me, before we entered his flat, that his mother was ill and would be a little frightened. The flat was dark but snug, and I found the rugs and ornamental objects attractive. Alex led me to a curtained doorway, eased the curtain aside and spoke softly to a shadowed figure propped up in a bed under a window. The cries of an agitated bird came from the bed as he approached, leading me by the hand. His mother looked at me in alarm, her cheeks trembling. She was old, but not ancient. After more gentle, placatory words from Alex, the old woman lifted a hand from under the covers and beckoned me closer. She studied my face in the grey light. We left the room after what sounded like a short, repeated phrase of approval or acquiescence.

In the tiny kitchen, Alex explained that his mother had been tortured during the war, and still suffered. The news filled me with awe. I said, 'The Germans?' Alex gave a bitter laugh. 'I'm afraid you don't know the history of this country,' he said. While he prepared an omelette, I asked about Yugoslavia, about Tito, about communism, but he was dismissive. I desperately wanted to ask him about his mother's torture, but managed not to. Why I should have wished to know baffles me now.

I slept on a mattress on the sitting-room floor. Every time I woke, I heard the bird cries of the old woman. Alex in his pyjamas stepped over me a number of times to go to her aid. I heard the soft, lapping phrases he spoke, his voice never rising. This must have been his task each night.

The train from Belgrade took me back over terrain I had thought was behind me. At least I was neat, once more. Hitching had left my green suit looking weary, but I had taken the opportunity at Alex's apartment to iron it, and also to shower. Shaving was still a few years off.

Hostel

I WAS MET in Athens by an official from the embassy – a good-natured kid who could easily have come from my own town – and taken to a modern building at the end of a barren boulevard. A more senior official looked me over, shook his head and told me that I would be on a plane back to Australia within two weeks. In the meantime, I was to be put up at a youth hostel, and I would pay my way by washing dishes. This seemed a dumb plan, but the two weeks would give me a chance to make a better one.

The hostel – a big, white, neo-classical monster right in the middle of the city – gave me my first real look at my own generation. And the thing I noticed was that all the other members of my generation were a lot more clued in than I was. They didn't wear suits; they wore jeans, rumpled shirts, sneakers. They were relaxed. They didn't hammer away at closed doors with mindless intensity. They knew what they wanted. They knew the geography of Europe. They used travellers' cheques. They carried their clothes in rucksacks. They had modest, practical plans that included a return to the cities and towns they'd come from. They had not come to search for a green island, but to photograph the Acropolis. They intended to smoke a little dope, go to bed with each other, get drunk, then go home and complete a degree in engineering or marine biology. They had sense, and they knew the way ahead. Next to them, I saw clearly for the first time how desperate my own plans were. It was as if I were once again floundering in the Myer Emporium, gazing hopelessly at all the jaunty folk who understood the code that was such a mystery to me.

At least I was employed within the limits of my competence. I knew how to wash dishes. They arrived in towering stacks from the mess hall, smeared with spaghetti and meatball left-behinds. Wrapped in a neck-to-ankle white apron (I couldn't seem to escape slapstick costumery), I stood at a deep sink and scrubbed the daylights out of anything passed to me. Warm, misty clouds enclosed me for hours. The rowdy rattle of hundreds of cheerful voices played in my ears like canned laughter.

When the mess hall closed and the chirruping throng had headed off to nightclubs, the kitchen staff gathered at a table to sip retsina and smoke and pair off for the night. Two of the waitresses, astonishingly pretty girls from Santa Fe, would head upstairs with the kitchen-hand they hadn't slept with the previous night. The kitchen-hands, Billy and Santo, accepted this turn-and-turn-about arrangement with nonchalance. Philly and Cassie did not consider taking me upstairs, but they did kiss me and rub their breasts against my cheeks and include me in a survey they were conducting, in a desultory way, about the advantages of various condoms.

In the late evenings it was left to me, as the sole employee with nothing to worry about in the way of birth control, to man the reception desk and register the herds of swaggering undergraduates who arrived on ferries from Brindisi. Each national group had a flavour. The Swedes rollicked and capered as if they'd just been let out for the weekend from a high-security venue of detention. The Germans were restrained, serious, as if conscious of the poor impression their fathers had made as tourists between 1939 and 1945. The English were good-natured and co-operative, but lived with a morbid fear of larceny. Australians, mostly girls, were even more co-operative than the English but didn't dwell on the prospect of having their pockets picked. Americans were easy-going, generous, embracing, especially the draft dodgers.

It was the fervent hope of the draft dodgers that the Vietnam War would come to an end before their visas ran out. Athens, located about as far from the United States as you could get without subjecting yourself to the discomforts of the Third World, was the ideal place to sit out the war. The youngest draft dodgers were only three years older than me, but seemed immensely more mature. I lingered close by whenever a group of them got together – sometimes in the mess, sometimes in the cafés nearby – and tried to look as if at any moment I might say something definitive about the role being played by the United States' armed forces in South-East Asia. The dodgers would glance at me, but didn't invite me to join in. Until one day. A tall, rowdy guy named Donny called me over from the shadows and got me to sit down beside him. He threw an arm around my shoulder and demanded to know exactly what the CIA was paying me.

'The CIA?'

'Yeah, kid. Whaddya getting?'

The half-dozen others were watching me through narrowed eyes.

'I don't get anything from the CIA.'

'Yes you do, kid. You get plenty. I seen you in a big, fancy restaurant down on Constitution Square. Seen you having lunch with George from the embassy.'

'I don't know anyone called George.'

'Yes you do, kid. You know plenty. George's job, you know what it is? George's job is to keep tabs on us guys. Seen you down there in Constitution Square with George, reading out of a notebook.'

'I wouldn't do that! I wouldn't give anybody any names!'

'Hoo! Now, I didn't say nothing about giving names, did I? That just popped out, didn't it? Think we got a stool pigeon here, my friends. Doctor Lubisch, if you'd just pass me the castrating knife? Sorry as hell about this, kid.'

'C'mon, back off, Donny,' he was told. And he did.

'Had you going there for a minute, right? Give us a smile. What's your name?'

'Bobby.'

'Bobby! Bobby's good. Every Bobby I ever knew was a sweet, sweet guy. I think I'm already in love with you, Bobby. But what the fuck are you doing here? I mean, what the fuck are you doing here? You're, like, twelve, maybe?'

I tagged along when the dodgers and their girlfriends went up to the nightclub district to eat and drink. It was considered important culturally to have sex on the Acropolis while the sun came up. A Jewish girl from Brooklyn, Deborah, wildly drunk, gave me a binding commitment to sex – but after she'd passed through the hands of Dean and Jerry and Wayne on the crumbling steps of the Temple of Athena, she'd lost her zest.

It was probably just as well. My observations of Deborah's demeanour in the throes of passion alarmed me. The women of the green island behaved in a well-mannered way, with gentle sighs, murmured expressions of thanks. Deborah was more forward. She thrashed about like an enraged eel and screamed obscenities at Wayne, at Donny, at Jerry. She drew the line nowhere at all. 'Fuck me, you cunt!' she screamed at Jerry. She slapped them, she spat in their faces, she pulled their hair. The dodgers took all this rough handling cheerfully and had no complaints to make when it was over and they were sitting with their arms around Deborah, passing a bottle of ouzo back and forward. Deborah herself became the plain, plump, good-natured young woman in horn-rimmed spectacles she'd been before sex. It was baffling to me.

As on the ship, I took what solace I could from books. Before I discovered the American Library at the back of Omonia Square, I read what was left about in the hostel – *Last Exit to Brooklyn*, *Mountolive*, *Franny and Zooey*. But it was finding the American Library that made my life vivid once more. Randall, a colleague of the dodgers but not one himself – he was in his early thirties and had served in the navy – took me down to the library and used his passport to check out the stack of books I'd chosen. Arms full, I wandered out into the sunshine and stood gazing about at the city with a smile on my face. My happiness bulked within me; it had a weight and density. I carried the pile back to the hostel and curled up on my bed.

Down at the Australian Consulate, papers had been drawn up and were awaiting my signature.

'Qantas. Singapore, Sydney, Melbourne. You pay back the Commonwealth government at a rate not exceeding twenty-two per cent of whatever salary you are paid when next employed.'

The consulate official, a kindly, gruff man with the seamed face of a die-hard boozer, offered me the papers to sign. When I said that I had decided to stay in Greece, he sat back in his chair, puffed out his cheeks and let out his breath in a way that made his lips flubber. Then he shrugged.

'Right-oh,' he said. 'You're the boss. Expect to see you back here in a bit, but. Need any moolah?' He took five hundred-drachma notes from his wallet and passed them to me.

'Pay me back when your dog has pups,' he said.

A crisis began to build a few days later. It drew its vigour from the sleet and wind of a sudden, surly day. Everyone stayed indoors and smoked the dope of a deft little Mancunian dealer who called himself Dicky the Rascal. Interior lighting was banned during the day, and the hostel by the middle of the afternoon was as dark as a cupboard. In every room on every floor, in the attic, in every secret place, little parties had started up – some by candlelight, some in shadow. In spite of the chill and gloom, the hostel pulsed with life. Dicky the Rascal and his girlfriend sashayed from room to room passing out tiny packages of foil-wrap twisted at each end and calling out in a trippy sing-song, 'Moving it, comrades, moving it!'

Given the job that night of collecting money for mess-hall IOUs, I went from room to room with a leather pouch around my waist and a pen and pad in my hand. I was the only person in the hostel with a job to do at that time of night. I was unwelcome, but tolerated. The hostel had become Rio – music, fumes, laughter, bongoes. People walked about naked with smiley faces painted on their behinds; couples made love and conversation in a cheerfully preoccupied way, barely allowing sex to interrupt a conversation, never allowing a conversation to sidetrack sex. Requesting payment for servings of spaghetti and meatballs from young women sitting astride their boyfriends, I developed a slight stutter. 'No, no, that's okay, I'll c-come back later.'

I completed my chore and turned in the very little money I'd collected to the warden, a weary man with mottled lips, always on the verge of being overwhelmed by two things happening at one time, let alone a hundred. I went to bed and lay there in a mounting fever of longing, sick in every organ and muscle, the skin of my body like a burning shroud.

Listening to the jingle-jangle of laughter and music, I had to ask myself what it was that prevented me joining in. I was younger than everyone else, certainly, and seemed even younger than I was, but this was a festival and nobody cared about my age. I could have been a ten-year-old dwarf with a monkey's tail and donkey's ears and I would have been happily embraced and fondled, if I'd given myself up to it. Nobody cared. But I couldn't give myself up to it. Amongst a hundred people, I felt I was the only one floundering. What Eden could I have more ecstatically conjured than this one? Libidinous, naked young women of a dozen nationalities flaunting their breasts and behinds as they crawled across the debris of pizza crusts and peanut shells to fetch the last of a bottle of Smirnoff: how much more inviting did an orgy have to be before I gave a whoop and hurrah and joined in? If I didn't want hedonism, what in the name of God *did* I want?

I didn't know, and so I read. One novel was not enough to overcome the pain and yearning and self-disgust. I read ten pages of one novel, ten of another, another, another, another, another. At first, the frenzied reading was no more than white noise dulling the sound of laughter, but gradually the stories took hold and I was drawn into a minor festival of my own. I went from the railway platform where Lane Coutell stood reading a letter from Franny Glass, to March staring into the eyes of the fox on the Midlands farm she shared with Banford; to the crewman complaining aboard the *Narcissus*; to Dangerfield, the ginger man, gazing down the Balscaddoon Road and out to the Irish Sea; to Atticus's office in the court-house, containing 'little more than a hat rack, a spittoon, a checker-board and an unsullied Code of Alabama'; to the first description of Hester Prynne, 'a figure of perfect elegance, on a large scale. She had dark and abundant hair, so glossy that it threw off the sunshine with a gleam, and a face which, besides being beautiful from a regularity of feature and richness of complexion, had the...'

Literature cannot replace love-making, nor should it, except when it has to. I read for hours. Rio died away. I woke in the morning with a couple of books pressed against my ribcage and four more on the floor beside me. I was instantly happy to see how much more of the six books still awaited my reading, but within a minute I was blue to my boots to think of what I had missed that night. I wept, sighed, went to work sweeping up the mess of carnival all over the hostel. I saw many of the people, now clothed, that I'd seen unclothed some hours earlier. None looked the worse for wear. They'd awoken in Eden as eager, refreshed and cheerful as if from a week's slumber on swansdown pillows.

Winter blew in a crowd of rowdy Dutch kids fleeing subzero Amsterdam for the slightly warmer south. Most of them were Provos – politically pissed-off renegades. The hostel staff didn't like them. They were forever sermonising, particularly about the Vietnam War, and the dodgers took exception to holier-than-thou dyke-pluggers running down the USA. Also, it emerged that the Provos biggest political coup was getting the town fathers of Amsterdam to distribute white bicycles about the city. It was an environmental thing. But it wasn't all that sexy. It wasn't the Black Panthers. The dodgers thought it stupid and boring. The Dutch proselytised a fair bit about the wholesomeness of condoms, which was aggravating to the dodgers. Not so much the endorsement of condoms, so far as I could tell, but the intrusion of pious protestant do-goodism into areas best left pagan.

All in all, the dodgers and the hostel staff felt it a good time to move on. Philly and Cassie packed their bags and headed off to Istanbul. Donny and the dodgers followed a few days later. I had no idea what my next move should be. But I would not return to Australia.

Randall, an ex-medical corpsman from the US navy, had developed a pitying interest in my case. 'Jesus, Bobby, what the fuck are you going to do? You can't work here forever, kid.'

'Get another job?' I suggested.

'Who the fuck would *employ* you? You're not a goddamned brain surgeon. Don't you think a million Greek kids can wash dishes the same as you? Do you think the Greeks are *importing* dish washers?'

'I got a job here,' I said.

'You got a job here because the guy who runs this dump likes to get in with the embassies. Embassy guys ask him a favour, he asks them a favour. He's probably got relatives in Australia, probably planning to send his grandma down there, wants some slack with visas. Something. He's got an angle.'

This was demoralising news. I'd thought that my diligence at the kitchen sink commended me. I decided to take up smoking to make myself appear older and more employable. I had a pack of Winstons I'd found in one of the dorms. Halfway through the first cigarette, I swooned and fell down. But I persevered, and by the evening I had it down pat. I put on my green suit and wandered down to a café to show off my technique in public. Randall was sitting at a table with a couple of English girls from the hostel.

'What the fuck are you doing?' he demanded.

'Nothing.'

'Gimme the cigarettes.'

'How come?'

'Gimme the cigarettes!'

I handed them over. He took most of the remaining cigarettes then returned the pack.

'Wasted on you. You're not even breathing in.'

'I am!'

'No you're not. This is Jo, this is Cathy. Jo, Cathy, this is Bobby. Robert. We're going to Kuwait with Jo and Cathy.'

'Pleased to meet you,' said Cathy, offering her hand. Jo seemed a little sceptical.

'The thing is,' said Cathy, a cheerful girl with black hair, a dead-straight fringe and bright cheeks, 'we can't really travel in Turkey and Iran without male company. Not really, from what we're told. You get *pestered*, sort of thing. We can pay your way, and you pay us back when we get to Kuwait. There are very *very* good jobs in Kuwait. You'd have to agree to pay us back, you know, *properly* agree.'

'I agree,' I said.

'How old are you, if you don't mind my asking?' said Jo, less and less comfortable the more she studied my face.

'Me?'

'He's twenty, nearly,' Randall put in quickly. 'Anything you want us to sign, that's fine with us.'

'Oh, we wouldn't dream of it!' said Cathy.

'I'll type something up,' said Jo.

'Jo's a secretary,' said Randall. 'Worked for some big shot. Seventy words a minute, is that right, Jo?'

'Seventy-five,' said Jo. 'Royal Dutch Shell.'

MY FATHER'S LOYALTIES are always directed to men. Women are adversaries. One friend's wife is a drunkard, and my father shakes his head in disgust when he hears what the friend has to put up with. He offers to talk to the wife, see if he can put her right. Another friend's wife is a notorious nag. Dad commiserates. Whenever he talks to me of holidays, of just getting away from everything, it's understood that he means getting away from Gwen and from women altogether. He speaks of camping trips up on Big River; maybe even going further, taking a look at the outback. You'd never want to take a woman with you on a long trip, he says. Women complain. They can't help it.

Thinking of what Dad has said, I realise that he must have in mind the big trip to Eden he made with five mates back in the days when my mum was still around. I remember him coming back from the coast with a couple of hessian bags full of fish and ice. He dumped all the fish out on the kitchen table — fish galore, slithery and gleaming. Lumps of ice clattered off the table and whizzed across the kitchen floor. Dad was as high as a kite. He and his mates, filthy and unshaven and smelling of fish guts, shook their heads and grinned, delighted with their catch. My mother didn't seem delighted at all. She didn't actually complain, but she looked put out. So I get an idea of what he means when he says you wouldn't want to take a woman with you on a long trip. They don't get happy in the same way as a man.

East

CATHY REMAINED CHIRRUPY the whole way to Istanbul. As the train battered its way through a snowstorm, I watched with delight as she sat with her nose against the window, rattling off a commentary. 'Ooh, there's this tiny, *tiny* village and a man with a donkey, I daresay he's a Turk, oh, and it's piled *ever* so high, this little cart thingy the donkey's pulling, he's utterly the loveliest thing, the little donkey – oh no! – I don't like that, I really don't like that, he's striking the poor beast, oh that is cruel, that truly is cruel!' Jo, pale and uncomfortable and complaining of the stench of her fellow passengers, seemed the least likely person to enjoy travel of any sort. 'Oh do shut up, Cathy! I don't want to hear about donkeys!'

The Turks in the compartment gazed at Jo only briefly, rejecting her with their eyes, but they followed Cathy's every motion closely. When she chattered away at the window, kneeling on her seat, they stared at her bum swinging this way and that as if it were a vision of indescribable mystery and enchantment. She spent a great part of the journey reading to me aloud from *Emma* and telling me exactly what she would be doing now if she were not in a train on the way to Istanbul but back in Sheffield. 'Firstly, washing Daddy's car, it's a Sunbeam, which might sound a little teeny for a family car but there's only the three of us. I do the mats, too, take them right out, scrub them, and then hang them on the line to dry.'

The people we'd known in Athens had re-established themselves in unaltered idleness in Istanbul. We found them all on the evening of our arrival, crowded into a cheap eatery in the oldest part of the city. Philly had sent back home for more money; she intended to study belly-dancing at an amazing academy in the shadow of Saint Sophia. Cassie was considering a career as a high-class whore. Wealthy Turks would pay any price on earth for a girl with cornsilk hair and pink cupid's bow lips. Seeing Philly again threw me into turmoil. Her beauty was overwhelming. Also, we communicated so well on an intellectual level. She read books, for instance, and so did I.

Cathy went missing for a week shortly after our arrival in Istanbul, and when we found her again, the soft red roses in her cheeks had been replaced by hectic flushes. The tender expression in her blue eyes was now smoky, lickerish. She had met Donny, who was finding Philly not quite to his taste. Cathy was in love, stoned, and her lips were swollen. She had taken on the job of hat-slut – she passed around the hat for Donny while he played guitar in various eateries. She had lost all interest in continuing the journey to Kuwait to work as a nurse, the profession for which she had been trained. Jo was furious. She set her lips in a thin, white line and glared out at the world like an irritated dormouse.

Meanwhile, Philly and Cassie had been visited by the father and mother of a boy who'd paid them a large sum of money for sex. The father and mother suggested that the money should be returned, because that would mean that their son had merely had sex with Philly and Cassie (not such a bad thing) but hadn't paid for it (a bad thing, to have paid for it). The girls gave back the money on the understanding that the same sum would then be offered to them as a gift, but this didn't happen. The incident ruined their vision of living in perfumed luxury on the Bosphorus, and inclined them to return to Santa Fe.

Listening to all this troubled me. It was not that my ideas about sex were gentlemanly; they were quite as salacious as the next boy's. It was just that the idea of lust in women, or a mercantile leaning, exposed the egocentricity of my sex plans. Despite all I'd read about sex and love and the hurly-burly of boy–girl relationships, I'd paid no real attention. I'd seen people in love; I'd seen people broken-hearted; I'd seen my mother weeping, before her departure; I'd seen my stepmother and my father transformed into homicidal maniacs by the disappointments of love. Why should I have believed that an island existed where warm-hearted women waited to devote themselves to my service? Weren't they *human*, these women?

Still confused, I left Randall and Jo at the hotel one cold morning and wandered around the city by myself, hoping to lose my distress in the creation of new, maybe more realistic, fantasies. I hoped to stumble across a harem, this being Istanbul. Some years earlier, I'd read a book about a girl called Angelique who, at the time of the Crusades, had wound up in the harem of Saladin. Angelique was blond, tender and sweet. She had endless sex with Saladin and was crazy about him, in spite of he being a Muslim and she a Christian. I was looking for a place where women like Angelique sashayed about in their underwear and tenderly ministered to boys who came in from the street.

I didn't find anything like it. The women I saw, those who were draped in shawls and those in Western dress, went about the normal business of women – working, or going to work, or shopping, or herding kids along, catching taxis, jumping off buses, shouting, chattering. But what I did find was something that increased my upset.

I turned into a narrow cobblestoned street where men were unloading crates from the back of a truck. The men were uniformly small, dark and haggard, like urban serfs, eternally ill-nourished and eternally over-worked. That was what made me stop to watch – the ground-down look of the men. Each wore a harness that supported a frame hanging from his shoulders. He would back up to the tray of the truck, bend over, and a crate would be dropped into the frame. In that bent-over posture he would stagger over the cobblestones, unloading the crate on the landing of a warehouse. The crates were very big and obviously very heavy. Fork-lifts did this work in my country.

The men were skilful, but the work was dangerous. And as I watched, an accident happened. A man slipped and fell. The crate he was carrying landed first on the cobbles, then rolled over on him, pinning him down. His workmates hurried to him, calling shrilly, like a flock of dark birds. They hauled the crate from him, supported his head, pulled his shirt up from his trousers. His face was white and his body twitched. Blood from a tear above his groin ran onto the wet cobbles and grew like a flower. I could see that his wound was terrible. The corner of the crate or the wire strapping had ripped across him. He was dead in perhaps a minute. People came from everywhere; they stood on any raised surface to get a better look. Two or three of his workmates hammered at the cobbles with their fists. The others stared down wordlessly. I could see that some ritual was about to commence, for a holy man, or so he seemed to me, was being ushered through the crowd. There was no sign of a medic or of an ambulance. I moved away a little, then kept moving.

After an icy draught of shock that set me trembling had died away, I tried to understand whatever it is we are meant to understand when we see a human being cuffed out of life in that way. And perhaps I did think about the poor man and his fate for a bit. But the dominating thought was not really a thought at all, but a great shift in the furniture of my mind. Perfumed boudoirs, soft beds, velvet drapes, the upholstery of Saladin's harem – all of that disappeared. The stage was now bare and echoing, with few lights.

Jo became the sole supporter of the expedition to Kuwait. She spoke of Cathy sometimes with sorrow ('I don't know what I'm to say to her parents, I'm sure') and sometimes with disgust ('The girl is a harlot, pure and simple'). She didn't need me any longer; Randall was her pretend boyfriend. She would certainly have suggested that I buzz off, but Randall wouldn't hear of it. 'Say I get sick, who'll keep the Arabs away from your arse? Bobby's our back-up.' Jo had no confidence in my ability to keep the Arabs away from her arse, nor should she have had, but she needed Randall and had to listen to him.

Jo's home life in Sheffield appeared to have been so cosy that it was difficult to work out why she ever felt the need to travel to Kuwait. On the long train journey to Ankara, she worked herself up into a Sheffield frenzy, chattering about the games she had enjoyed with her dad in the evenings. 'At chess, of course, he was a master,' she told us. 'I honestly had to give up trying to beat Daddy at chess. Do you know, sometimes he would give me his queen after the second move, and I still couldn't beat him? Cribbage was a different matter. A different matter entirely. You'll think I'm boasting and I can't help it if you do, but at cribbage, at least with Daddy, I was supreme. Do either of you play cribbage?' I gave the impression of being interested but Randall couldn't be bothered. 'For fuck's sake, cribbage?' Jo, with her anorak tied up under her chin, blushed pink, but persisted. 'I do think we might try a game of five hundred. I have the cards with me. There's nothing to see out the window, surely.'

'I'm going for a piss,' said Randall. 'You coming, Bobby?'

Once in the corridor, Randall took me by the shoulders. 'She's driving me crazy,' he said. 'Can you fuck her?'

'Pardon?'

'She needs a fuck. What do you think she's here for? I can't do it. I tried to get interested in Istanbul, but I couldn't. You do it. She'll be okay after a fuck, for a while.'

'Okay,' I said.

'Take her into the john.'

'The toilet?'

'Yeah. Do it now.'

'But it's dirty!'

'The john? Who cares! Do you think she cares? Do you care?'

'There's not enough room to lie down!'

'Aw for fuck's sake! You don't lie down, you moron! You stand her up!'

'Stand her up?'

'Okay, forget it. Cribbage. Jesus Christ.'

Randall was in too bad a mood for me to ask him about the thing that was troubling me so much, which was the problem of unequal distribution of wealth within a society. The dead haulier, crushed by the crate, returned again and again, his face white on the wet black cobbles and the blood trickling as if a small tap below his abdomen had been left running. I wanted to be happy. I wanted to concentrate on the beauty of women, on their breasts and lips, and the way they nonchalantly pushed their hair back from their faces. But if people like the little hauliers had to make a living as they did, how could I concentrate?

I didn't know how much of my uneasiness to accept and how much to forget. Randall might say, 'You can't do anything about it, it's the way it is, that's all.' Or he might say, 'So what? The guy had an accident.' I needed a hand. The problem was strangely shaped. I needed help in making it rest properly on a shelf. People should have more money than the little haulier had. Why did they *not* have more money? The question seemed exactly that stark. It would never again seem so stark. Books, knowledge and life would offer explanations, but never quite shake my conviction about the bald, bothering, *badness* of such injustice.

We found a tiny hotel in Ankara, on the verge of a vast, ashy wasteland more or less in the middle of the city. The desolation dragged Jo down into a slough from which she could not rise. She sobbed to herself and squeaked incessantly. Randall, tired of the squeaking, went out for a walk in the freezing evening air and returned ill. He took to bed and shook. His experience in the naval medical corps allowed him to diagnose pneumonia. 'Get some money from Jo, find a pharmacy and buy this.' On a piece of paper he wrote 'Acramyacin'. Off I headed into the sour city, clutching the paper and the money.

Ankara looked joyless and dull. Ill-will sat on every face I saw. Blunt, brutish buildings reared above sites of desultory commerce. I found a pharmacy – not so easy, because I was looking for a red cross. The bored pharmacist glanced at the scrawled word and asked me in impeccable English whether I had the authority to administer antibiotics. I said that I had, and he immediately handed me the medicine, charged me an insignificant fee and said wearily, 'Get the dose right, for your patient's sake and mine.'

Back at the hotel, Randall dosed himself and crawled back under the thin blankets. His shaking was so violent that the iron bed danced its way first left, then right. After Jo and I had eaten a wretched meal of soggy beans and lard in the world's least welcoming restaurant (perched as it was above the ash heap), I attempted to seduce Jo – as a favour to Randall.

'You look lovely tonight.'

'What?'

'You look lovely tonight.'

'Oh do shut up. I feel dreadful.'

'Yes, but I was just saying that you look lovely, even though you feel, you know, dreadful.'

'I despise this country! I despise everything about it! For pity's sake, just do look at these wretched Turks! I've a mind, you know, to pack it all in and go back to Britain.'

'Oh. Well, it's their country. They're allowed to look however they like.'

'Don't start that. Cathy was always going on like that. God, that imbecilic girl! In all fairness, it was a jolly drab thing she did, you'll agree with that.'

We tramped back to the hotel. I'd done my best. Jo cleaned her teeth (an assiduous ten-minute scrub, the brush applied in five distinct formats), pulled her blankets over her head (we all shared one room) and began to sob. I put my blankets on the shuddering form of Randall, dressed myself in almost every garment in my suitcase, and slept in bundled comfort.

Randall was no better in the morning. His face had a dull, silvery look. He allowed me to dose him and to help him to the toilet down the corridor. 'If I get any worse,' he croaked, propped above the feculent hole, 'call the goddam embassy. You got that?'

'Yep.'

'What do you do?'

'Call the embassy.'

'What's happening with Jo?'

'She's feeling dreadful, and crying.'

'Yeah. Well. Keep sweet with her, Bobby. She pulls out, we're fucked. Play cribbage with her.'

I played not cribbage but five hundred with Jo. I enjoyed it. I used to play with my stepmother, a bitter and intense opponent. Oddly, the game brought out Jo's generosity. She was a hopeless player and always lost to me, but would gleefully relay the results to Randall. 'Honestly, you would not believe it, you would *not*! I was four hundred and fifty, Bobby was nil, and what did he choose? Open misère! Five hundred points in a single game! Not even I have *ever* done that!'

The antibiotics cured Randall in a week. He was touched that I'd given him my blankets, and pleased about the impact of the card games on Jo's mood. He told me, in a way that filled me with pride, that I was only half the idiot he'd always thought I was. It was important to me to have Randall's endorsement because he knew about books. He'd already read most of what I was reading. I had kept most of the books from the American Library in Athens, compensating it with a number of my own that had fallen in my esteem. It was fair. My books were in better shape than the library's. When I was struggling with *Tender is the Night*, Randall told me not to bother, that the book was a dud. I put it aside and started on a collection of Isaac Singer stories, and was given a little approving nod of the head by Randall. I wondered how a medical corpsman in the US Navy had become so well read, but I didn't dare ask him. Some months later, re-reading *The Nigger of the Narcissus*, I came to Conrad's observations about the reading habits of sailors, and showed it to Randall.

'Bullshit,' he said. 'Never knew anybody in the navy who'd read anything.'

'What about you?' I said.

'I was just passing time in the navy,' he said. 'Mostly, I'm a genius.'

It was marginally cheaper to travel by bus than by train, and Jo insisted that we save every penny we could. The buses were all bone and sinew; no upholstery, no comforts of any sort. We found ourselves in regions of Turkey that seemed entirely populated by hillbillies. The men wore daggers at their waists. Their skin was the colour of sandstone; their hair flamed with henna. The sight of Jo in jeans incensed them.

In the bare little towns, posses of men would follow us, picking up handfuls of dirt and stone to throw at our backs. Jo, who was given to fits of English melodrama, told Randall that he was to kill her if they attempted to rape her. He assured her that the men were probably far more interested in me than in her, so far as rape was concerned. 'Rubbish!' she said. 'Men don't rape men!' Randall went on to explain, in a scholarly way but not without delight, that Muslims were not much into rape. Stiff penalties were prescribed, and in any case the men would be offended by her unshaven twat and, without knowing when her last period had finished, would be reluctant to touch her. 'They practically have you surgically scrubbed before they'll go near you. Bobby's different. Sweet little arse like that. You take a look around next time. It's Bobby's arse they stare at.' Jo, crimson with embarrassment, went into a deep Sheffield sulk and wouldn't talk to either of us until we reached Tehran.

 Apartment

AS THE NUMBER of travellers' cheques in Jo's wallet grew fewer, her mood worsened. A highly directed anger took the place of sobbing and squeaking. She asked questions she intended to answer herself. 'What possible job could Bobby do in Kuwait? Well actually, I have the answer to that. He'll do nothing. For example, he has a typewriter and he can't even type. But he can wash dishes. Oh, wonderful! He can wash dishes! And what of my other star boarder? He's also well equipped to wash dishes. Well, let me tell something to both of you. You *shall* wash dishes! You shall jolly well wash every dish in Kuwait until I have back each last penny I've advanced you! Each last penny!'

After one of these outbursts – this one in Tehran – Randall soothed Jo by encouraging her to speak of her plans for the next few years. She liked to do that. And so she sat on the side of her bed, fixed her eye on a patch of floor and spoke in a maniacal whisper of the large sums of money she would make in Kuwait, of the chaps she might meet, of the romance that might be kindled down there on the Persian Gulf, of marriage, of children. Randall had already told me not to ask questions of Jo whenever he set her off on one of these fantasies. I might have asked her was why she didn't work hard and make a large sum of money in Sheffield, and get married there. But then, why hadn't *I* stayed in Australia and found a nice girl? Why was *I* sitting in a hotel room in the bustle of a huge Iranian city pondering my chances of meeting a nice Kuwaiti girl on the Persian Gulf?

Or Randall – what about Randall? He'd confessed to me only the day before that his situation was desperate. We'd been searching for a bar in the middle of Tehran, and hadn't found one because there weren't any. The only bars were in expensive international hotels. So we drank pomegranate juice and sat on the sidewalk, and Randall confessed that he was as blue as he could get. 'Why? Why do you think? I'm thirty-two, I'll be thirty-three in a couple of months. I've got nothing, no wife, no kids, never been married, not a dime to my name, nothing. Now I'm sliding along on the skin of my arse to Kuwait! Fucking Kuwait! I've gotta *do* something. I'm not a fucking kid. For you, it's okay. You're ten years old. This's nothing, this's just, what? – an adventure for you, whatever. I'm thirty-two, Bobby! I've gotta *do* something!'

'I'm sure you'll be okay,' I offered. 'You're still young looking.'

'Oh, great. Now I'm getting encouragement from a ten year old.'

'You could marry Jo.'

'Are you *completely* insane? Marry *Jo*? Just tell me to kill myself, how about? I'll jump out there under the next truck. I'll tell you one thing. If she mentions 'Britain' once more, I definitely *will* kill myself. She doesn't even say 'England', she says 'Britain' – 'Boo hoo, I'm going back to Britain'. Christ, the fucking English are pathetic, just fucking pathetic.'

The wait for our Kuwaiti visas stretched out. The Kuwaitis were in no hurry to embrace us. Keen to show my worth to the expedition, I headed out one morning with my typewriter to see if I could find a day's work. My idea was to set myself up on a park bench and offer to type up letters in English for Tehranis with relatives in America or Australia or wherever. I'd seen men working at this craft in Istanbul, hunched over ancient Smith Coronas. The shortcomings of my project were not apparent to me. Why would Tehranis wish to send a letter in English to their relatives? How would my clients convey the substance of the letter to me unless they could speak English themselves? And so on.

My project was not much of an advance on the money-making schemes I'd employed in my home town. I sold snake-bite kits: a used razor blade, a length of string. You opened the snake bite with the razor blade then made a tourniquet with the string. I packed the blade and the string into a little metal HMV gramophone needle-case. I'd found a hundred empty metal cases up at the tip. My asking price for the kit was ten shillings – pretty steep. I attempted to hawk the kits to fishermen down on the river bank, and to tourists. I didn't sell one. Other schemes included hiring myself out as a black-tracker, even though I was white. But I had terrific success with less ambitious projects. I sold mudeyes, worms and yabbies to fishermen; went door to door as an odd-job boy; rooted through the debris at the tip retrieving soft-drink bottles. So for all I knew, my typing plan might have worked.

Tehran was not a city of parks. I found no park bench, no picnic table at which I could set up. But I did find a tiny strip of grass beside a highway, and there I settled with my typewriter beside me on top of a pile of paper. I wrote a sign, 'LETTERS TYPED IN ENGLISH 50 RIALS PER PAGE', and displayed it to the passing traffic. I was wearing my green suit.

People stopped to stare, but not to dictate a couple of pages to a distant relative. I was ready to give up after a barren hour or so. Then a smartly dressed officer of some sort (army intelligence, as it turned out) in starched, pale-green twill wandered up to me, smiling, and asked a great number of questions, none of then related to my new craft. Hearing that I was filling in time waiting for a visa to Kuwait, he rolled his eyes and gestured with his hand toward the sky. 'Kuwait very bad. Bad people,' he said. He was handsome, in his thirties, with a thick, highly groomed black moustache. I thought he was running some sort of racket, but what the racket would be I couldn't imagine. When he suggested that I, together with my friends, stay in the apartment of a man he knew instead of wasting money on a hotel, I immediately agreed. He wrote down his name and the address of the apartment, gave me three fifty-rial notes for the taxi fare, and arranged a meeting for the late afternoon.

Randall was impressed when I gave him the news. Jo wanted me to recall every detail of this Captain Mahsood Zamamzadeh's appearance and behaviour. She feared that he would rape her. In the end, for the sake of the savings, she agreed to go. Mahsood met us at the apartment and showed us inside. It was completely bare, although clean and obviously expensive.

'Blanket,' said Mahsood, waving a hand at the floor. Then he said, 'In kitchen, food.' He shook hands with each of us and promised to return in the morning. He locked the door when he left, and was gone before we could protest.

We found a white paper bag half-full of sugar in the kitchen, but nothing more. Jo believed that Masood was going to bring back a dozen of his friends to rape her.

'Why a dozen?' Randall asked her, irritated. 'Why not one, or two, or five? Why a dozen?'

'I just know,' said Jo. She made us sleep snugly wedged against her, she and Randall in sleeping bags, me in my blue cabin blankets.

Captain Mahsood did not come back with a dozen friends, but he did come back alone. 'Food,' he said, and with a big white smile handed over a crumpled brown paper bag that contained perhaps a dozen raisins. He had also brought a guitar. He sat down cross-legged on the floor and sang 'Love Me Do', accompanying himself, poorly, on the guitar. 'You now,' he said, and handed the guitar to Randall, the only one of us who could play it. He sat tuning it for five minutes, then sang 'The Streets of Laredo' in a beautiful, piping tenor. It was my turn. I sang 'From a Jack to a King', with Randall on guitar. Mahsood was delighted and sat smiling like a lunatic. Jo refused to sing anything, and instead demanded to know why he had locked us in. 'Safe for you,' he said.

We were free to wander about during the day, but were instructed by Mahsood to return at six in the evening. We did so, that evening and the next three evenings. The apartment had no electric power, so we sat around my candles reading, chatting, speculating on Mahsood's motive. Between Jo and me, an unspoken rivalry had developed. Each of us hoped that Mahsood would make a pass. Neither of us wanted to satisfy him, but each wished to be the one to say, 'Certainly not.' Jo had ceased to believe that she was likely to be raped, and was prepared to say one or two nice things about Mahsood's appearance.

The high point of my relationship with Captain Mahsood came when he turned up one morning with some flour for us. It was part of a packet of O-So-Lite flour from my native land, but with Farsi script on the bag. It made me cry. The high point of Jo's relationship with the captain was reached when he violated her in the kitchen. She emerged in a rage, her face its characteristic crisis crimson. 'We're leaving!' she said. Mahsood stood in the kitchen doorway with his head bowed and his peaked cap in his hands. 'Sorry please!' he said. It was later revealed that he had kissed Jo on the top of her head.

We lost our free lodging, but at least Jo was in a good mood for the remaining days in Tehran. She heaped curses on Captain Mahsood, deplored the conduct of all the people of the world who had not been brought up in the British Isles, and generally radiated goodwill. She allowed Randall and me to buy cigarettes for the first time in two weeks. We loved the captain.

Bus journeys in Iran imitate, in sluggishness and discomfort, progress by camel or donkey. It is by preference, I think. Drivers relish the sudden, unanticipated thud into a dip. As the passengers rise towards the ceiling, a communal shout of merriment is followed by guffaws of rough delight. I guessed that they were recalling famous lurches and dips of the past.

All the passengers were poor. If you had money, you found some other, sissier means of travel.

I was still brooding in an off-hand way on the fate of the little haulier in Istanbul. Being surrounded by poor folk on the buses was, I thought, good for me, good for my soul, and maybe even good for the world, since I was using my time to brainstorm. Desalination, for example. Huge desalination plants on the coasts of poor countries, piping limitless clean water to desert regions such as those outside the bus. Biscuit factories turning out a super high-protein, super low-cost snack. My compassion lacked the vital complement of disinterest. I wanted the poor to benefit in order that I should benefit. The Nobel Peace Prize gold cup gleamed in the crystal cabinet of my imagination with all the lustre of the Nobel Prize for Literature gold cup.

The poor of Iran flattered my sense of humanity (one of the time-honoured functions of the poor), but I missed the sight of girls – their bare arms, the swell of their breasts, the definition of their lips, the swing of their hair. The strictures of Islam had been successful in smothering the beauty of the Iranian female form under a noggin-to-ankle vestment. T. E Lawrence believed that the war against the sensual was Islam's way of countering sexual incontinence. In my homeland we studied America as closely as any country on earth, and so knew that sexual incontinence is practically a citizen's obligation. I had grown up besotted by the beauty of the female form – what could be more natural? – and was encouraged in my delirium by the spells and incantations of almost every hawker in the land. My heaven was populated entirely by women so emphatically mammalian that you could not open your mouth but that a nipple thrust its way in.

All of this, Islam denied me. I was travelling in a part of the world where I was *least* likely to see a naked breast, *least* likely to cover a kissable mouth with my own. The women I saw – on buses, or walking about towns – were busy being mums, or busy being girls who would pretty soon be busy being mums. And they were excellent mums, endlessly enduring, endlessly affectionate mums, but they were not the stuff of my dreams. In any case, they had no interest in me.

The chaps – that was a different story. I was having enormous success with the chaps. Just as Randall had promised, my arse was exercising a fabulous allure. I was felt up on crowded streets, in queues, in shops. On buses, the hand of my neighbour might creep towards me by slow degrees, then fall, seemingly by gravity, onto my thigh. The jolting of the bus might bounce this hand onto the pudding of my groin. The surprised hand might find within its grip the fly fabric of my green suit pants. I would remove the hand, gently returning it to its owner, who might give an embarrassed smile.

More difficult to deal with diplomatically were the frotteurs. Hemmed in left, right, front and back in a crowded shop, I would become aware that the gent behind me was quietly attempting to winkle his betrousered dick into the crack of my bum. I might move a little to the left, and so might he. Or I might turn side-on, only to find myself claimed by a new neighbour. I might turn and scowl, and meet a blank face, ignorant of my intended complaint. Or I might mutter, 'Oh for God's sake!' and storm out of the shop. Or I might simply sigh and roll my eyes and murmur to myself, 'Okay, make it quick!' – and shoot him a venomous look when I finally claimed my bread and cheese and hustled back to the bus. One morning in Isfahan, I thought 'Enough is enough!' I swung around, and stared down at an ancient dwarf bollocking away furiously at the back of my knees.

Randall sympathised with me, consoled me, but his essential interest was scholarly. 'To these guys,' he said, 'you're a slut. You're from the West, you wear tight pants. As far as they're concerned, you're begging for it. If you were from here and you dressed like that, you'd get whipped, probably. They think you don't know any better because you're a Christian. You're no loss even if they fuck you to death.'

'I'm not a Christian,' I said. 'I'm an atheist.'

'Doesn't matter. All that matters is you're fuckable. You can't fuck your girlfriend here until you marry her. You're next best. Get used to it.'

Jo, disgusted with men, with Iran, at first held herself aloof and wouldn't listen to my tales of woe. But then she became interested.

'Do you let men put their thingies in your bottom?'

'No! Jesus, Jo!'

She didn't believe me. She thought I protested too much. She went about with a smug, knowing air, very like my stepmother Gwen when she accused me of being 'sly'.

When I was left in peace, I tunnelled into my books as into a cave of buried treasure, forgot the world and spent hours marvelling over jewelled goblets and fat golden coins. Returning to the local at intervals, I gazed from the window of the bus at the baked desert, at canyons of clay and treeless

valleys, at towering formations of rock as bright as the flesh
of carrots. Within the swelter of the bus, children slept across
the laps of their mothers, their heads lolling, bubbles of spittle
forming at the corners of their mouths. Men drowsed in their
seats or fingered prayer beads, their chins raised and their eyes
fixed on paradise. A woman who had let her shawl fall onto
her shoulders quickly and expertly wrapped her head again
after catching my gaze. Raw onions were passed between the
members of a family, the skin tossed to the floor. Always a
few old men of great piety stared out the window as they
recited the endless cantos of a poem of praise to the Almighty,
pausing at intervals to wipe tears from their eyes. A child might
suddenly appear before me, balanced in the aisle of the swaying
bus, black eyes of stunning beauty scanning my face,
pondering the mystery of a boy dressed in this way with *Lolita*
resting in his lap.

The names of the towns we passed through were not
displayed, as they would have been in Australia. A little way
out of Isfahan, I asked a little boy to tell me where we were,
using the few words of Farsi I had picked up. 'Mahyar,' he
said, then for the rest of the journey to Shiraz he trotted back
up the aisle each time we came to a town, his eyes dancing in
delight: 'Shahreza... Sular... Aminabad... Shurjestan... Deh
Bid...' Sometimes he would act out what the town was known
for, putting his fingers to his head and waggling them in
imitation of a goat, or raising his hands high as he stood on
tiptoe to indicate a famous mosque.

He made me understand, with clever actions, that he
required the name of the country I had come from. 'Australia,'
I said, three, four, five times, changing the stress, taking care

with the pronunciation. But he couldn't get his mouth around it and obviously had not heard of it, and was happy only when Randall whispered to me to me, 'Say America', which the boy had heard of, of course. 'Decks Us', he said, pleased with himself. And brandishing an imaginary Colt .45, 'Argon Smock. Pow pow! Maddy Lon.' (Where would he have seen *Gunsmoke* in Iran?) And taking real trouble, 'An Angry Force,' which surfaced from my eddies of puzzlement as 'Niagara Falls.'

A little girl came down the aisle one evening and, instead of staring at me, held up her arms. She was asking to be lifted, held. Her mother, looking around the corner of her seat, gave a little shrug and nod of her head. I dropped my novel to the floor, hoisted the girl onto my lap, cradled her, and she fell asleep within minutes. An hour later she was still asleep. The pain of supporting her in the one position was awful, but the aching merged with a sort of daddy delight in providing comfort. Whenever she stirred in her sleep and looked up at me and smiled, happiness spread like a pleasant ache through my chest.

Past Shiraz, heading west to the Persian Gulf, we entered a night made more intensely black by the pillars of fire roaring above the oil wells. Gas was being burnt, and its reek mingled with the suffocatingly humid air, so that it seemed the bus was penetrating deeper and deeper into a swamp on the frontier of hell. The roar of the gas thrummed through the bus, waking the children from sleep. Like me, they stared out in alarm and excitement at the radiance of the fires gilding the ridges of the barren hills. The little boy hurried up to tell me that we were coming to Abadan, and turned an imaginary steering wheel left and right, acting out the destination of petroleum. He wished to know if I would go to sleep in Abadan (hands to the side of his head, eyes closed briefly). 'No,' I said. 'Kuwait.' 'Kuwait?' he repeated, and wrinkled his nose. 'Bad!' he said.

LIKE MOST WORKING-CLASS men of his generation, my father first travels beyond the shores of Australia as a soldier. In 1941 he is sent to Palestine with the 8th Battalion, AIF. He is twenty-three years old, but is thought to be much younger. He learns to drink, and finds he enjoys it. Cross-legged on the floor of a bar in Jaffa, he sings all night, urged on by his mates. He has a clear tenor voice and has picked up a little vibrato trick that kicks the cowboy songs along; he has also mastered a Jimmy Rogers Tennessee yodel. He sings 'Mountains of Morne', 'Danny Boy', 'Galway Bay', 'The Rising of the Moon', 'Road to Mandalay', 'Goodnight Irene', 'So Long, It's Been Good to Know You', 'Farewell' and 'Always'. He also recites. He has 'The Man From Snowy River' down pat, and 'The Face on the Bar-room Floor', but the piece that drives his audience crazy and wins him free drinks until morning is 'The Shooting of Dan McGrew'.

His mother, whose picture he carries in his breast pocket, taught him all the songs he knows, and the poems, too. He has no picture of his father. His father is a bit of mystery, dead for some time now. He better recalls his stepfather, a true bastard's bastard who used to tether him by one hand to a fence post and larrup the daylights out of him with a horsewhip. And for what? For nothing.

Later in the war, he sings and recites in Trincomalee, Moresby, Milne Bay.

After the war, he has a lot to say about the women of the islands, of course, but the people of the East have also left an impression. 'You get nothing out of Bob Arab,' he tells me, 'but bullshit.' All the men of the East are Arabs in his stories. 'Hates the old white man, the Arab,' and 'Treats his wife criminal, an Arab will.' He holds that the wartime crop of Arabs are a different breed than the Arabs of the Crusades, many of whom (but by no means all) were capable of behaving with great dignity in battle.

My father's stories of the East don't convince me, unlike his stories of the green island. The dismissive tone of his Arab reports makes the world seem smaller; his stories of the green island are like a sea breeze that fills a sail.

 Kingdom

OTHER THAN JET planes, the only transport to Kuwait from
Abadan was the dhow, the ancient craft of the gulf traders
with its lateen yard and sinewy hull. The dhows of the Tigris
were mastered by tall, disdainful Arabs. They had no curiosity
about us. The master of the dhow we approached refused
even to look at us. He asked for a sum of money, modest
enough, through another member of the crew. When we
agreed he said 'Hup!', and snorted and gestured over his
shoulder for us to come aboard. Only then did he turn his
gaze on us. He shrugged in contempt and spat into the river.

The boat's real cargo was lettuce and artichokes in crates
piled high above the gunwales. Randall, Jo and I were expected
to sit on top of the crates. The crewmen, running barefoot
over them, never missing their footing, swore at us and cuffed
us aside when we got in the way. Jo, who seemed to relish
opportunities to inform the insolent of her rights, stood
cawing, 'I say!'

Just for a bit, out on the blue-black waters of the Gulf, sailing
for a small kingdom of fabulous wealth, I forgot all about
girls – didn't worry whether their breasts would be big enough

and soft enough, whether they would love me, whether (my new anxiety) I would be burly enough for them, exciting enough. I was free to be thrilled by my good fortune. I could have been sweating over a boiler full of offal in the backyard of the butcher's shop, but instead I was scooting across the Persian Gulf with a sunrise as bright as blood staining the sky. The wind pushed the sail; the sea rushed along the hull with a soughing sound. The master of the boat stood erect at the long spar of the tiller, with a cigar as thin as a pencil bitten between his front teeth. I was suddenly aware of *width* – of how far life stretched to each side, rather than just ahead.

We came to the city of Kuwait by stepping out of the dhow. In the Kingdom of Kuwait there was only Kuwait, and we were in it. A dozen tall buildings, a glistening highway between them, spruce emporia, many small shops of the roll-down-door sort, two or three gorgeous five-star hotels, a number of flop houses and a few venues of hospitality between five star and flop. It was not immediately obvious what role I might play in the commerce of this instant city. I had vaguely thought that I would become an oil company executive, and would probably need to obtain a driver's licence for the Cadillac that would go with the job. But all the Cadillacs in town were being driven by hip-looking Arabs in highly laundered white robes. There was no evidence that kids from Australia were being shown to luxurious office suites by local millionaires, and asked to sign important documents. Quite the opposite; these crisp Arabs looked at the three of us as if we were puddles of mud that might splatter their immaculate clothes.

We found a hotel, not as cheap as in Athens or Istanbul. No air-conditioning. Randall lit a cigarette and looked out the window on to a not-very-bustling street. 'This,' he said, 'is a fuck-up.'

'Well, if it is or not,' Jo shrilled, 'you both of you get out there and find a job!'

'Where?'

'I don't know! On an oil rig! They have oil rigs here, don't they?'

We left Jo sobbing in the hotel and wandered out to find work. Randall asked a suited Kuwaiti the way to the hospital, where he intended to offer his services. The quality of the medical training he'd received in the navy had convinced him that he was in a better position to render services to the sick than any GP. Unfortunately, some Kuwaiti bigwig was receiving treatment at the hospital and the place was ringed by armed guards. Nobody at all was being admitted until the bigwig was cured. I suggested that we head back down to the dock and offer ourselves as labourers.

'Jesus, Bobby! *Labourers*? Open your fucking eyes! Every country in the Middle East is crawling with Palestinians. You know how much they work for? About a buck a year. Labourers!'

I didn't know that. I didn't know about the Palestinians. I didn't know anything about the Middle East except the few things Dad had told me. Nevertheless, I wished to prove that I was not the drop-kick that Jo thought me. I searched assiduously for work. I wandered the streets of Kuwait looking for any 'Help Wanted' signs that might happen to be written in English. I didn't find any. But I met a number of Kuwaitis who were keen to take me to bed. Their approach to boy–boy sex was different to the Iranians', who had less money to spend than their Gulf neighbours. The Kuwaitis offered money outright, according to the capitalist ethic. When I said no, they shrugged, as if I were incapable of seeing a bargain when it was staring me in the face. I didn't hold it against them.

On one of my excursions, all attired in green, hair neatly combed, I was offered a well-paid job as a farmhand by a prosperous-looking citizen who spoke English.

'I have a beautiful farm. In Kuwait, the most beautiful,' said Mister Ali.

'With grass and things?'

'No grass.'

'Cows?'

'A goat. Very beautiful.'

'What job do you want me to do?'

'Feeding goat. Each week, one hundred pound Kuwaiti.'

'Okay.'

Mister Ali drove a white Pontiac convertible with red leather upholstery. I took a seat beside him and he roared out of Kuwait on Highway 1, into the desert. The Kuwaiti desert looks exactly as a desert should look: flat stretches of sand, dunes, and low, barren hills. It was early evening when we reached his farmhouse, a cottage that had apparently been plucked from the Cotswolds and airlifted east of the Great Nafud. It was surrounded by a green picket fence. It was the only house I'd seen since we left the city.

Mister Ali blasted the horn loudly on arrival, and jovially invited me to give a honk or two as well. As we stepped out of the car, a stooped little man hobbled out of the house to greet us.

'Servant,' said Mister Ali with a laugh. 'Name, Hussain. You say, "Hussain".'

'Hussain,' I said.

'No, no! Say again, "Hussain".'

'Hussain,' I said once more, this time getting the stress right.

'Good! Soon all we speak Arabic. Ha ha!'

Mister Ali's geniality suffered a brief lapse while he addressed Hussain. It appeared that he was giving an order that Hussain didn't wish to carry out. Mister Ali grew hot under the collar; Hussain made faces and scowled and snorted. But Mister Ali seemed finally to prevail, and Hussain went off with ill-will on bandy legs to do as he was told.

'Very funny man, Hussain, ha ha!' said Mister Ali, cheerful once more. 'Jelly Chub Land!'

'Pardon?'

Mister Ali put a finger under his nose and tottered up and down, bandy-legged.

'Oh,' I said. 'Charlie Chaplin.'

We sat at a table on the verandah. Mister Ali screamed to Hussain once more. Hussain appeared, carrying a bottle of Johnny Walker and two glasses on a tray. He put a dish cloth around the bottle before setting it on the table, then grimaced with distaste before toddling off, mumbling discontentedly to himself. I worked out that he had not wished to touch the bottle with his naked hand. What Randall had told me about the disdain of the strict Kuwaiti regime for alcohol was surely true.

After pouring two large, neat glasses of Scotch, Mister Ali took up a canister of what seemed to be pepper, and created a thick, black cap on each of the drinks. He demonstrated how to drink through the filter of pepper. I took a sip, found the taste vile, but did not betray anything.

'Where's the goat?' I asked.

'Goat?' said Mister Ali. 'Ah, goat! Yes. Goat coming.'

But the goat didn't come. Mister Ali urged me to finish that first glass of Scotch, then poured a second. He treated his own drink more lightly. Hussain shuffled out from time to time to express his disgust, but disappeared when he was screamed at. The desert all around was soundless.

'Are you,' I asked Mister Ali, for want of conversation, 'a millionaire?'

'Money?' said Mister Ali. 'Hoo! Very much! Very very much! US dollar. Sterling. Swiss Franc. Very much, very!'

I began to feel ill. My eyes couldn't focus. Mister Ali was kissing my hand and wrist.

'You,' he said, 'so thin, so white!'

I thought, Oh Christ!

Mister Ali kissed my cheeks, and buried his face in my neck. His bristly moustache dug into my flesh. I couldn't imagine how women could bear such a thing against their skin.

'Gotta go,' I said, struggling to my feet.

'No, no, stay here, all the time you only with Hussain and goat, nice for you!'

'Gotta go.'

Hussain stood on the verandah with thunder on his brow. A screaming match broke out. Mister Ali was plainly furious, and so was Hussain. I felt so sick that I thought I would kill Mister Ali and Hussain, then take the car. I wanted a doctor or an ambulance. Mister Ali, however, seemed to lose the argument, and he and Hussain got me into the Pontiac.

Mister Ali took off with a shriek of tyres and zoomed down the highway at phenomenal speed. As the headlights of oncoming cars reared before me, I took it for granted that we would crash and that I would be killed without ever having reached the green island. I wished to sob, but was too sick to do so. Mister Ali, one hand on the steering wheel, was feeling me all over and kissing me passionately. 'So thin, so white!' sounded in my ear like the lyrics of a pop song. I was conscious of the smell of whisky and of the humid aroma of Mister Ali's cologne. My priority was to stay alive. When Mister Ali dived his head down to my groin, I was enraged at his disregard of the rules of safe driving and slapped at him wildly. He straightened himself in time to avoid a Detroit massacre, and drove the rest of the way into Kuwait City a bit chastened.

Too ill to move, I had to be dragged from the car to the hotel. Mister Ali propped me against a wall, jumped back into the Pontiac and hit the accelerator. A small crowd gathered around me. My stomach, as if waiting for an audience, heaved everything through the air. A couple of men from the hotel helped me upstairs, admonishing me all the way. 'No go with Ali! Bad, bad man!'

Jo studied me with fascinated contempt, as if I had met with the fate I so richly deserved. Randall did some doctoring, wondering aloud if there were anything I would not do to demonstrate my stupidity. 'A *farm*? Do you know how many farms there are in Kuwait, you moron? Zero! Zero farms!'

The working-class culture in which I was reared consigned all able-bodied young men who did not roll up their sleeves and work for a living to a special circle of hell. 'Wouldn't work in an iron lung,' my father once snorted, speaking of a boy of eighteen in our town who seemed to be taking a very long time to recover from a broken leg. Other sinning boys 'wouldn't think of getting their little pink hands dirty', or would 'drop dead from a day's hard yakka.' And so, the day after the farm debacle, I went hitch-hiking in search of oilfields and work.

Highway 1 rolled out into the desert, past Mister Ali's cottage and on and on. As soon as I stuck out my thumb, I was offered a ride by a German chemical engineer in a Mercedes. He guffawed at my plan to find work on the oilfields and advised me to return to Australia as soon as I could. He dropped me at the intersection of Highway 1 and a Bedouin camel track, promising to pick me up and take me back to Kuwait if I were still there in two hours. I dismissed his advice and pressed on for the oilfields. What did he know? He wasn't Kuwaiti.

The next car that stopped was driven by an army officer – a general, to judge from his insignia. His face was pitted with pock marks, and looked exactly as spooky as skin does when magnified. He spoke no English, but asked with hand signals where I was going. On the side of the road I acted out the job of a man working in the oilfields – dig, dig, dig with my spade – and phew!, wiped my brow. The general watched me impassively, then gestured for me to get into the car. As soon as I was seated, he made a U-turn and headed back towards Kuwait City. I reconciled myself to making another foray into the desert the next day.

He took me to a shack on the outskirts of town. Four walls and a bed. I realised immediately what would be offered but – courteous as ever – I knew that I should wait for the offer before refusing it. Some of the best-mannered children ever released to the world were, I think, bred in my little patch of rural Australia. The general sat on the bed with a heavy sigh – he was fat and wheezy and not in very good health, by the look of him. He patted the bed beside him, and I sat where he'd patted. He took a wallet from the inside pocket of his khaki jacket, drew out a number of notes and placed them one at a time on the tartan blanket. He had the deliberate movements of a man who has never been required to show haste in anything. I gazed with remote distaste at his profile, at the pendulous lower lip mottled with unwholesome blue smears, at the dense stubble that ran down into the gullies of his chin and neck.

'You,' he said when he was ready. It was his only English word.

'Me?'

'You,' he said again, and stared at me in his unfocused way out of lustreless black pupils.

I suddenly noticed that he was pointing at his crotch. Leaning back on the bed and trying to stare down his chest past his belly, he unbuttoned his fly. An enormously fat penis lifted its head from the folds of khaki. As we both gazed down at it, it began to grow, vegetable-like, as if its arousal were being displayed in time-lapse photography. When it had reached its full state of engorgement, its diseased condition became more obvious. It had the texture and colour of a pineapple skin. The general, in dumb-show, gave me to understand that if I were to take it in my mouth, the money on the bed was mine. I declined with a shake of the head. He looked at me regretfully for some time, then slowly nodded as if, after some thought, he'd come to see my point of view.

He packed his dick away, brought his hands down on his thighs with a long exhalation of breath and wheezed himself to his feet. Then he drove me back to the hotel.

I didn't tell Randall and Jo about the general. I told them that I'd attempted to hitch to the oilfields, but hadn't made it and would try again the next day. They themselves had been struggling to find work. Randall had consistently been turned back from the hospital; Jo had failed to place her shining references under the scrutiny of the big shots at the oil company offices. We should, all of us, have been demoralised. Instead, Jo and Randall listened to me quietly, nodding at the wrong places, seeming not much upset about things. I was too puzzled to feel relieved (I'd feared a tongue-lashing from Jo). Then I noticed Jo's knickers peeping out from under the pillow. The stud of her jeans was not secured. Randall's belt was unbuckled. They'd dressed hurriedly, hearing me on the steps. I'd been out searching for work and they'd been having sex! I felt betrayed, instantly. Particularly by Randall.

'S'matter?' asked Randall, seeing my frown.

'Nothing.'

'Aw, c'mon! Something's wrong.'

'You know as well as I do!'

'Huh?'

'I'm going out.'

'Bobby! Hey, pal?'

'I'm going out!'

I snatched up one of my unread books and stormed out. I didn't slam the door behind me, but I did close it pretty firmly.

It was even more pointless to look for a nice little park in Kuwait than in Tehran. No parks, no grass. I ended up standing on the sidewalk, reading. An old woman wandered up to me and asked me something, over and over. I later came to know that the word she was using meant simply 'What?' as in 'What gives?' I finally lost patience and told her that in *my* country, people were well-mannered enough to permit another person to read a book on the sidewalk without being bothered by, by – *stickybeaks*! But I wasn't actually reading my book. I was going over and over the script of my grievances with Jo and Randall. I mean, what was the use of me bursting my boiler, if, if – oh, it was just appalling their behaviour, *appalling*!

Eventually, I had to go back to the hotel. Jo and Randall looked chastened, as they ought. I made a barbed remark about hoping that my arrival had not inconvenienced them too much. Jo, in unguarded moments, looked sickeningly smug. Also, she began wandering around in her underwear – something she would never have done before. She wasn't all that bad looking in her underwear, in fact. By the time we gave up on Kuwait and left to try our luck back in Shiraz, I was fantasising about a short, ill-tempered English girl in gingham knickers who had no interest in me other than as a bonded debtor.

A HOTEL OF astonishing luxury once stood on a street teeming with people buying and selling from market stalls. My father spent two nights in one of its elegant bedrooms during the war. The hotel had been taken over by the Australian army. That stay was my father's only experience of luxury in his life, although he does not use the word 'luxury' in describing the hotel's splendours. He speaks of it as 'posh, like a palace'. He normally uses 'posh' as a term of mild disdain or contempt, referring to affectation (Nigel Harrison's letterbox, for instance, which, alone of all letterboxes in Eildon is adorned with big, brass numerals). But when he says that the fabulous hotel was 'posh', he is simply trying to do it justice. Its reception desk was carved marble; its staircase was made from a similar stone, only pink, or pinkish. The carpets were a thick, red plush. Framed paintings were everywhere, even in the bedrooms where they could easily have been stolen.

In my father's bedroom, which he shared with five comrades, a huge painting of a ruined castle hung above the bed. The painting wasn't a copy or anything like that; it was an original. You could feel the paint with your fingers. The bathroom was enormous, almost as big as the bedroom, all tiled in designs that included what Dad at first took to be swastikas but which turned out only to be swastika-like symbols of a sort found all over the country. And in the enormous bathroom, what do you think? A bed! The idea was, apparently, that you would take a bath, hop out, dry yourself, then stretch out on the bed while a servant brought you tea and biscuits. You pulled a long sash thing to call the servant, not that there were any servants when my father was there.

You open the window and the shutters, and what do you see? A million people, blacks, scurrying about in the street below, and a bay as blue as the sky, incredible. You wouldn't find anything as posh as that hotel in Australia, not Sydney, not Melbourne, nowhere. Do I know why, my father asks; and when I don't know, he explains. 'No coolies in Australia. For a hotel like that, you need coolies, cheap labour. White people won't do it.'

But posh. Really posh.

 Hotel

DOWN IN THE bazaar, a few days after we arrived in Shiraz, three tall men in dusty black robes and turbans caught my attention. They looked straight ahead as they marched along the narrow lanes, expecting people to step aside, and the people did step aside. Each of the men was followed by a line of women dressed head to toe in black. The women's faces were hidden by studded leather masks. Some women didn't have much of a spring in their step, and so I took them to be older. Some seemed to be very young, perhaps in their teens, although I couldn't be sure. The women of each group were tied each to the other with cord. I could see their flickering gaze as they passed. I thought I could discern curiosity in their eyes, even liveliness. But in the eyes of the men, there was no curiosity. Their chiselled, fleshless faces were models of haughty derision. If they found their way blocked, perhaps by a man leading a donkey or a merchant with his back to them, they simply stopped and let their gaze wander a little left and right, like gunslingers in a crude western. The women would come to a lazy halt, bending a little as they laughed, as if they could see the humour in all this arrogance. The market-goers and

143

merchants were not dressed in robes, but in jeans and shirts and pullovers. I noticed smiles on their faces – satirical smiles. These tall haughty men and their wives were hicks and, although they were spooky, they were also absurd.

I learned some time later that they were tribespeople down from the hills for a day. Shiraz, I was told, brought five thousand years of history to life in one day. Western culture was welcomed by the Shah's régime, up to a point, and the middle-class girls in skirts and blouses who sauntered along the boulevards had embraced the West as firmly as was permitted. The poor held on to what was more familiar. The tribespeople were not so much fundamentalist Muslims as ferocious Muslims. The clerical class of mullahs, liberals and conservatives alike, were pissed off with the leaching away of their authority that came with the encroachment of Western values and fads. The intellectuals loathed both the Shah and the mullahs.

My sole question, addressed to the quiet, amused and witty man who was attempting to educate me was, 'If you convert and become a Muslim, can you still have four wives?' I wish I had craved to learn more about the tribesmen; I wish I'd owned some real curiosity about the world. But when I arrived in Shiraz, it was still the same old thing: scrounging for love.

We had no money and nowhere to stay when we stepped off the bus in Shiraz, but Randall struck up a conversation with a stoned Peace Corps couple who were prepared to let the three of us camp in their flat for a week. They were off to the east of the country, where hashish that had been cured according to the arcane rites of a mysterious desert sect was due to be dug up and sold for a song to whoever happened to be standing around. The flat was fine, but its cupboards were bare.

Jo became hysterical, but was taken under the wing of a fierce old man-hater at the British Council, a woman who thought it a shame that a well-brought-up gal like Jo should be forced to share a flat with two aimless boys who'd sponged her last penny. Randall walked down to what looked from the outside like a Middle Eastern version of St James Infirmary, and had the good fortune to meet a surgeon who'd been trained in his home town of Boston. The surgeon promised Randall a job, but had to renege when it was revealed that Randall had only a tourist visa. Leave the country, Randall was told, get yourself a six-month work visa, come back, scrub up, and into the operating theatre with you. But a six-month visa would cost a lot of money. Randall didn't have a zack. My own employment prospects were, of course, very poor.

Randall became for a while as hard to get on with as Jo. 'Know where I'd be if I'd stayed in the navy, Bobby? Would've been roster chief at some base hospital, could've just about had my choice, could've been *running* a fucking hospital! Had my own house on base, kid in school. What happened? Fuck, what *happened*, Bobby?'

I listened, but knew enough to keep any advice to myself. It might have been hunger that was beginning to mess up poor Randall's mind. We went three, four, five days without a bite to eat. Hunger gave a hypertonic edge to the sense of smell. The aromas of the street – roast kid, fresh bread, a spiced stew sold in BYO tin cups – curled into the nostrils like a hook devised by a genius of pain. I could pick up the wafty smell of nuts roasting a block away. Walking past a house where something delicious was being prepared, I had to fight down an insane impulse to force open a door and demand a bowlful of food in the name of the Australian government.

The time came, as it had to, when I was forced to consider the option of outright prostitution. In common with some millions of brothers and (especially) sisters down the centuries, I decided to deny my left hand a clear view of what my right hand was doing. I shuffled down to a big café on Boulevard Pahelvi, stood about looking famished, accepted an offer of hospitality from two well-turned-out gents, gobbled down a huge plateful of something, then faced up to the job.

The job was to be undertaken in a bath-house on the outskirts of town. I was hastened there in a big flash car as soon as I'd finished eating. One of the gents spoke a lavish brand of English, the other spoke not at all. In the warm, stewy mist of the bath-house cubicle, I passed my skinny body into the hands of my patrons.

'Hmm,' said the English speaker, 'a very bony fellow you are, ha ha! But you are a nice boy. Shall I call you Robert or Bobs? What is your custom?'

'Bobby,' I said.

'Ha! Bobby! Hoo, a delightful name!'

The second man, the taller and more imposing of the two, seemed to be watching on with a certain amount of unease. When the English speaker went to work with soap and lather and practised hands, his friend turned a little away, and frowned. I must have shown some stubbornness, because the tall, silent man suddenly broke his silence and barked out something not in Farsi but in Arabic – I could tell the difference. An argument followed.

'This is for money,' the English speaker said to me. 'For money, hokay?'

'No,' I said.

'But you are always fucking boys?'

'No,' I said.

The tall man glanced at me, then averted his eyes. He spoke in Arabic again.

'For thirty pounds, Kuwaiti pounds,' said the English speaker. 'The same as sterling pounds.'

'No,' I said again, but with a helpless sense of ruining a meal for me and Randall at the five-star Parki Saadi hotel. I didn't know why I was ruining things. I could probably have survived without too much toiling and moiling. I felt fed up with myself.

And so it came to an end. A slender boy and two older men standing around in the mist with nowhere to go. We dried ourselves, dressed, I was driven back to town. We parted with a handshake.

Freshly laundered as I was, I suddenly thought of walking up to the Parki Saadi and asking for work. This was an optimistic plan. The hotel, set on acres of lawn on top of a hill above the town, was the Ritz of southern Iran. It set a standard of luxury that took in such details, so it was said, as a multiple-slice toast-making machine that would have been considered fabulous even in the classiest hotels of Paris or New York. The owner was a wealthy playboy who kept the hotel as a hobby. Down at the market a few days earlier, I had noticed a tall, contemptuous man in Parki Saadi livery walking around the stalls and barking out orders to a squad of lackeys. He, it appeared, was the buyer for the hotel's table. The grovelling obsequiousness that the stall owners displayed when the buyer stopped before their stalls was very impressive. I would have liked his job, if the hotel thought of offering it to me, but that didn't seem likely.

As I wandered in through the hotel's ornate wrought-iron gates, I decided that I would offer myself as a sort of maître d', hobnobbing with the English-speaking patrons and asking in an affected British accent if anything at all might be done to enhance the pleasure of their stay.

Once or twice in life we become, briefly, a project of the angels. They muster about us invisibly, read our thoughts and, for the sake of the amusement it offers them, grant our wishes. I wandered into the gorgeously upholstered lobby of the Parki Saadi in rumpled shirt and trousers, asked the concierge if I might have a word with the manager, and was shown into a classy suite where music was playing softly on a stereo. I outlined my hobnobbing plan while Ahmoud (as the manager insisted I call him) listened with sage goodwill. He asked me if I had a work visa. I said no. He opened a drawer in his desk and handed me a thick wad of fifty, one hundred and five hundred rial notes. I was to travel to Basra in Iraq, obtain a work visa, return to the hotel and commence my career in the hospitality trade. Did I have a suit? Ahmoud's hand slid towards the drawer once again. Oh yes, I said – I certainly have a suit. Ahmoud rang for the concierge, filled him in on his plans for me and instructed him to show me to the restaurant.

I left the hotel an hour after my arrival with my pockets full of money and a magnificent three-course meal under my belt. I tottered blissfully back into town, purchased bread, bananas, lollies, apples, rice pudding, cigarettes and beer, and had the whole lot of it spread out on the floor when Randall arrived back at the flat from his own hopeless quest for food and work. He was flabbergasted. And the sum of money I had been given was enough to cover his fare to Basra, too. He could obtain a work visa himself and start work at the hospital. 'How the fuck did you do that?' he wanted to know. Later, he requested that I allow him to take charge of the wad of notes. He spoke with tact and sensitivity, but it was pretty plain that he thought the money would disappear if I were left in charge of it. I said 'Sure'. He wept, and told me that I was a good kid and not really an idiot but just – well, it'd be better, wouldn't it, if he kept the money safe on the journey?

It was, I think, a shock for Ahmoud when on my return from Basra he saw the green suit. I'd had it dry-cleaned, but a certain shabbiness had overtaken it. Also, I seemed to have undergone a growth spurt over the months of travel and the trousers, already short, now hung shorter. I recognised that I didn't entirely look the part, but what I lacked in style I was determined to make up in the sophistication of my banter with the international guests. The guests were mostly French. They would naturally wish to converse with me in their native language. It was therefore necessary for me to learn French in a hurry.

I found a second-hand French primer in a bookshop on Boulevard Pahlevi, and went to work. It wasn't long before I'd mastered the present tense of the verb 'to be', which seemed to me the heart and soul of the French tongue and almost all I would need to know of the language. 'I am happy.' 'I am sad.' 'I am tall.' 'I am good.' 'I am sick.' And best of all, the killer application of the verb, 'I am at your service.' The French guests, however, in their haughty way, insisted on straying all over the place in their use of the language. I would listen attentively to words vaulting and spinning, then smile my most ingratiating smile and tell them that I was at their service. Eyebrows would be raised, and the guests would sensibly suggest that I speak to them in English:

'Are you enjoying your meal, sir?'

'Yes.'

'May I offer you some biscuits?'

'Thank you, no.'

'Will you remain long in Shiraz?'

'A week.'

'Will there be anything else?'

'No, thank you.'

A regular task was to type the menu each day. At this I was adept – I had my own typewriter, after all. But I had not yet learnt how little patience there is in the general population for the gratuitous flourish. I added quotations and fragments of poems at the bottom of the menu. Hemingway was a favourite. Chekhov didn't lend himself to pithy quotations so well, and even I was aware that one or two of the Chekhovs were a little too protracted for a menu: 'Mamma! Are you crying, Mamma? My dear, good, sweet Mamma! Darling, I love you! I bless you! The cherry orchard is sold; it's gone; it's quite true. But don't cry, Mamma, you've still got life before you, you've still got your pure and lovely soul...'

One morning after I'd presented the menu to Ahmoud for his okay, he pursed his lips and looked up at me from his desk. He always wore sunglasses. It was not possible to read anything from his eyes.

'What is this part?' he asked, tapping the quotation with the top of his fountain pen. The quotation that day was, I think, a paragraph from *Death in Venice*, with Aschenbach expiring on the beach and Tadzio pointing to the sea and the horizon. I'd thought it thrilling, and deep.

'Thomas Mann,' I answered.

'No more,' he said, and it was clear that he meant it. Typing the menus became a boring chore after that.

Small disappointments aside, the job was terrific. I sat reading behind the front desk all day long. Breakfast, lunch and dinner were provided for me. I ate like a king. Whenever I strode across the lobby in my green suit, the porters and cleaners smiled and salaamed. My confidence grew. I became bold enough to flirt with Ahmoud's wife, a breathtakingly beautiful woman who'd been raised and educated in Paris. She called me into Ahmoud's office one day when he was off somewhere, and asked me to zip up the back of her dress. She kept a rack of dresses in her husband's office and it was her habit to change whatever she was wearing a number of times each day. She was holding both hands in front of her, fingers pointing up.

'My nails are wet,' she said. 'Hold up my hair. Be careful.'

Once I'd zipped the dress, the single most exciting experience of my life to that point – the pink bra-strap, the fragrance of her shoulders, the weight of her black sheaf of hair – I stood more or less at attention awaiting further instructions. She was leaning over the desk with her back to me, reading an article in a magazine and wiggling her fingers in the air. I knew I should do something, show some initiative, but was at a loss as to what initiatives were at my disposal. A few weeks earlier, I'd kept my mind off food for hours at a stretch by listening to Gilbert and Sullivan – the only record in the apartment. The refrain of one of the songs went, 'Faint heart never won fair lady.' I'd puzzled over the words and had asked Randall for help. 'Women don't like it if you act shy. You've got to come on.'

I placed my hand on Ahmoud's wife's behind, which was inclined towards me as she bent over the magazine. I didn't caress her behind – I merely let my hand rest there while I stood beside her, still at attention. She gave no indication, even that I was still in the room. She continued to wiggle her fingers, leaning further forward now and again to turn the pages of the magazine with her elbow. Whenever she moved, my hand registered the exquisite flexing of her muscles. I would have been happy to remain where I was for months or years. Ahmoud's wife turned and looked at me over her shoulder. It was a lazy look, as if a long and languid process of thought had just concluded. A tiny smile, not quite scornful, played at the corners of her lips. She reached around and took my hand off her behind, then tapped me on the tip of the nose with a single outstretched finger. I silently returned to my desk.

My head was full of the delicate fragrance of her perfume. I believed myself in love with Ahmoud's wife and could relieve my longing only by repeating beneath my breath, 'I would die for you, die for you, die for you...' My reverie was interrupted by a voice asking in a coolly amused way if I was making progress. It was a tall, graceful man in his early thirties whom I had seen about the hotel quietly handling documents, occasionally making a note in a ledger. He was standing beside me now, studying what seemed to be a sheaf of accounts. He was smiling at the sheaf of papers and only switched the smile to me when he was quite ready.

'A little progress?' he said.

'At what?' I asked.

'My assumption is that you are attempting to seduce Parivash.'

'Me? No.'

'Oh, then I apologise for my mistake.'

He put down the papers on the reception desk and gave his name as Houshang. 'It's a beautiful day. Walk with me,' he said, and slipped on his sunglasses. I followed him out into the hotel's garden. He didn't turn around to check that I was following him, even when he began a monologue on flowers.

'Shall we sit here?' he said, when we came to a rose bower arching over an ornate iron bench. He took off his sunglasses and reached for a rose.

'Parivash will not sleep with you,' he said softly. 'She will not sleep with you because you are far too young. Also, she is very faithful to her husband. There it is.'

'Oh,' I said.

'I will find you a nice American girl. Or a French girl. Do you speak French?'

'Yes,' I said, then 'No.'

'No?'

'No.'

'It doesn't matter. A French girl or an American girl. We will go to Persepolis the day after tomorrow.'

Houshang, as I came to learn, was the drop-by accountant for the hotel. He turned up once every couple of days, confirmed by glancing at the books that Ahmoud was spending much more money than the hotel was taking in, then went back to his job at Iran Insurance in the city. His employment at Iran Insurance was no more taxing than his work at the hotel, so he kept up a third job, as a guide for wealthy tourists visiting the ruins of Persepolis an hour or so from Shiraz. The three jobs helped to keep boredom at bay. Driving with him to Persepolis in his second-hand Buick, he confessed that he was a poet trapped inside the body of an accountant. (This was, I learned much later, not an uncommon complaint of accountants.)

'Very little that Houshang dreams will ever come to pass,' he said, with infinite sadness. 'As for the young man Robert, perhaps his dreams will be waiting for him at Persepolis, perhaps not. It all means nothing, nothing. Houshang's life, Robert's life, the life of a flower, who could say which means more to God, or less?'

I quickly understood that my role in Houshang's life was to pronounce amens, which I did, mostly by nodding or shaking my head or even by sighing. I didn't care what he believed about his part or my part in the scheme of things. I only cared about the promised American girl.

All the tourists at Persepolis were women. All the women were French or American. Their husbands were diplomats or oil company executives who had reached that point in their careers (according to Houshang) when movement between sites and cities takes the place of tedious employment at a desk. Nothing was accomplished on these visits to sites and cities;

it wasn't expected. Motion signified everything. The greater the number of conferences attended or ministers visited, the less time spent back in Lyon or Paris or Philadelphia or Washington, the more apparent their dedication. By the time they had reached this career level, they had acquired children, usually two, and the children sometimes accompanied them. Wives often travelled with their husbands but, with nothing much to occupy them, they got fed up and had sex with Houshang.

My understanding of sex, attraction and seduction was limited, but even I could see that Houshang's allure – that of the sorrowing poet – would be lampooned to death where I came from. The class of women that Houshang tended were nonetheless dazzled by the sorrowing poet thing, or pretended to be. His line was so corny that when I first heard it, I blushed. It relied on imagery of efflorescence, often bordering on the obscene, and roped in all the great Persian poets. He spoke of the melancholy of the rose, he spoke of transience, he spoke of tenderness. And he unblushingly suggested that the true Persian knows that love is fleeting yet extraordinarily important, and that Western women, despite their liberty and ambition knew, too, that love and the rose are fragrant but briefly. 'Please do not let me embarrass you,' he would murmur in conclusion. 'You must say so if you are embarrassed.' They were not embarrassed. They were delighted, and moved. And in their delight and empathy, they permitted Houshang liberties that were, to me at least, breathtaking.

His client on that first visit to Persepolis was a tall, graceful woman in her forties, her attractiveness just a fraction marred

by an oven-fired look. When Houshang took her off to show
her something to do with Alexander the Great, I was left with
the daughter, Patricia, teeth strapped into shining steel braces.
When she smiled, it was like looking into the slots of a pop-
up toaster. But I liked her. She acted as if she had known me
all her life, and had an attractive bossiness. She used the word
'ludicrous' in every second sentence. 'My dad's, like, don't
eat anything that doesn't come from the hotel kitchen? – which
is ludicrous because I'm frankly not even *at* the hotel for ten
hours at a stretch. Robert, your pants are, well, too *short* for
you, did you know? Just stick to jeans, mostly. I met another
Australian. You're not like him.'

Patricia took it for granted that we would kiss. Her braces
made it awkward. The tongue recoils from stainless steel.
Standing against a pillar in the blazing heat of the sun, I
assumed that she was as embarrassed by this difficult and
joyless smooching as I was, and gave her lots of chances to
break it off. But no, she seemed delighted. She held her arms
around my neck and squeezed with all her might, or else
worked her fingers into the flesh of my back through the fabric
of the green suit jacket. When she did finally call it off, she
became her normal businesslike self. Later, I realised that her
enthusiasm had not had much to do with me. She had been
practising; ironing out glitches with someone who didn't
matter for the future benefit of someone who did.

Houshang and Patricia's mother eventually reappeared,
Houshang looking nonchalant, Patricia's mum a little over-
composed. He explained to me on the way back to Shiraz that
he normally made love to his clients right there at the ruins.
He kept a number of nooks clean and comfy for this very

purpose. He complained that making love always left him feeling sad but, as far as I could see, the weight of his sadness rested comfortably on a plump cushion of hearty self-approval.

Later trips to Persepolis did not afford me much relief from loneliness and hunger. The American daughters, when they were available, were usually unwilling to interrupt the perfection of a bored-to-death expression just to grapple with me. The French girls were much more interested in Houshang, and seemed to consider him wasted on their mothers.

Up in my neat little room on the second floor of the Parki Saadi, I lay in bed at nights struggling with the mess not only of the past few months but of the entire seventeen years of my life. My essential query was this: 'What the hell are you doing here? Iran? Why?' I rescued my sanity with narrative, by amending my yarn. I decided to fall in love. I was not trawling the earth for sex; I was trawling the earth for *love* (so the new version of my story went). And I had been driven to travel to Iran because I would find the girl who was meant for me, the one girl I could marry. *I was in Iran because it was meant to be.* There is no more potent element in autobiography than this.

I went further. I typed out the story of the love affair I would have liked. The story was called, 'Meant To Be'. The principal female character, an exceptionally tender-hearted young woman, had for years harboured a secret desire to win the heart of a young Australian travelling in Iran. It was an Australian boy she wanted – not an American, not a Frenchman, not a German, but an *Australian*. She herself was Iranian. She was a stewardess with Iran Air. Houshang had told me that the only respectable Iranian girls who slept with men before marriage were Iran Air stewardesses. This suited me, because Iran Air stewardesses stayed at the hotel between flights. They were cheerful girls, very saucy. Parivash was the name of the stewardess with whom I fell in love.

It was the custom of Iran Air stewardesses, once they'd been taxied from the airport to the hotel late at night, to meet up with the men they'd just finished plying with food and drink on the flight from Tehran – men who were also staying at the Parki Saadi. If a man didn't have the freedom of his suite for one reason or another – he could be travelling with his wife, for instance – then the meeting would take place somewhere in the gardens of the hotel. I didn't know all this. Houshang explained it to me later. What I *did* know was that the stewardesses often wandered down to the lobby after checking in. So on flight nights – Mondays, Wednesdays and Saturdays – I remained at the reception desk until very late, re-reading *For Whom the Bell Tolls*.

Six stewardesses served on the Tehran–Shiraz route. They wore smart navy-blue suits with above-the-knee skirts and jaunty little caps. Much of their good cheer and cheekiness was bravado, as I was to learn from Houshang. A peasant girl who had lost her virginity before marriage had no option other than to become a prostitute. Lots of such women worked the highways in and out of Shiraz, always dressed like any respectable housewife: head-to-toe black shawl. A middle-class girl or a daughter of minor aristocrats could either go abroad for a very long time and maybe marry a non-Muslim, or she could join Iran Air, if she were pretty enough. The stewardesses kept a sharp lookout for a European man to marry, Houshang said. I saw the injustice in all this and said so. Houshang shrugged and closed his eyes briefly, a familiar expression. 'Who can say? Indeed, who can say?'

The hotel lobby at midnight was a very quiet place. A few guests from the flight would check in and go to bed. The only night-life in Shiraz was enjoyed by members of the National Police and the Shah's secret police, who would hobnob at private houses where they drank themselves sick and told stories of the torture of communists and clerics – according to Houshang. In the tomb-like silence of the foyer, I would hunch over my book, waiting for the opportunity to fall in love. Or I might gather up the desk equipment and make a little design or a toy town using the stapler, sticks of staples, rubber stamps, ink pad, pens and pencils.

Whenever the stewardesses appeared, they were in a hurry. They crossed the lobby rapidly in their high heels and were swallowed by the night. They might murmur 'Salaam' or 'Hi', but they did not stop to establish a relationship. The first stewardess to talk to me was not named Parivash but Peggy. She was Canadian. She had short red hair and dense discs of freckles on each cheek. She asked me for a cigarette and suggested that I was a little young to be out in the world alone. I asked her how come she was working for Iran Air. Listening to her explanation, I revised my story about falling in love with an Iranian girl. In the deftly composed new version of my story, I fell in love with a Canadian girl on a hostess-exchange program.

After chatting to me for ten minutes or so, Peggy was met by an astonishingly handsome Frenchman whom I'd checked into the hotel a half-hour earlier – together with his wife and two sons, not yet in their teens. He was one of those superbly accomplished charmers who never bother to tone down the glow, no matter if the beneficiary of the radiance is boy, girl, grandma, child or beggar. He had spoken to me in French earlier but, finding me unable to respond, had switched to English.

'A young man of Australia? A country of great beauty. *For Whom the Bell Tolls*. Mister Ernest Hemingway. A superb writer. You have read others? I place him in the top rank. The front door remains open for a little while yet? Wonderful.'

Two nights later, I was compelled to revert to my original love story. One of the genuine Iranian stewardesses came down to the lobby and chatted. This one called herself Moo Moo, a name that lacked the magic of Parivash. She was pretty, certainly, but her eyebrows met in the middle, forming one thick arc. I wasn't crazy about the eyebrow, but I was sure I would get over it. She was nervous, and kept asking about the condition of the gardens. Were there things out there she might trip over in the dark? No, I promised her, nothing at all to trip over. She reluctantly ventured out into the night. Once she was gone, it suddenly struck me that she had been asking me in a roundabout way to accompany her. I bolted out the front door and into the gardens, searching high and low. The more desperately I searched, the more certain I was that I loved Moo Moo. I loved her big thick eyebrow. I loved everything about her. After searching for an hour all over the gardens, hearing nothing but the chirruping songs of crickets, I went wretchedly to bed.

Next day I told Houshang about Moo Moo. It turned out that he'd slept with her a number of times. Tousling my hair, he explained that Moo Moo had a drinking problem. Had she been carrying a shoulder bag when she went outside? Yes, she had. Well, that shoulder bag would have contained a bottle of Raki, Moo Moo's spirit of choice. She would have polished off the bottle, re-entered the hotel by the kitchen door and gone up to bed. She had terrific powers of recuperation and would have made the Shiraz–Tehran flight that very morning. Moo Moo probably would have slept with me if I'd escorted her into the garden, Houshang said, but there was no point in falling in love with her. Besides, she was already married to an Egyptian Christian who sold fake Rolex watches in Tehran. He promised me once again that he would find me a nice French or American girl.

TWENTY-FIVE YEARS after her departure from my life, my mother flies
to Melbourne from the city in which she's been living all this time to
be reunited with my sister and me. It is winter in Melbourne. My mother
wears a red overcoat, but not the one in which she left.

It is the initiative of my sister that has brought about the reunion.
My father is too tired and frail to care much if we invite our mother
back into our lives. Marion had placed advertisements in newspapers
far and wide. 'Contact your daughter. Love forever.' And a telephone
number. By chance, my mother sees one of these advertisements.
She responds, books an airfare, and so we meet.

I recognise my mother at the airport before she recognises me.
Her hair is white and abundant. The drama of the red overcoat is in
keeping with the intensity of her beauty. The gaze of her black eyes
rests on me, turns away, takes in my sister who has dissolved in tears,
then returns to me and my five-year-old son, pressed to my hip. We
embrace and kiss. 'Dear son,' she says.

My mother grips my wrist so fiercely in the car on the way back to
St. Kilda that I wince in pain.

We drink tea in my apartment. My sister cannot stop her tears.

'I want to hear everything,' my mother says. 'Leave nothing out.'

I summarise the years that followed her departure. When I speak of
travelling, of the ship, of my arrival in Greece, she asks in a puzzled
way how old I had been at that time. When I tell her, she says that it
was wrong of Frank to have allowed me to do such a thing. 'I wouldn't
have let you,' she says. 'And what did you do for money? Did you have
a job?' Yes, I tell her. I taught in a college. Without ever having known

me in those days, my mother realises immediately what a ridiculous figure I must have cut as a schoolteacher. She raises her eyebrows, seems indignant, as if she had been overruled in her opinion all those years ago. I don't remind her that she had not been in a position to intervene.

Before I have time to complete the story of my search for the green island, my son's mother arrives to take him back to her home in Coburg. He lives there most of the week; on the weekends, he stays with me. It is an arrangement that the three of us — my son, my wife and I — are still getting used to. My son finds it particularly difficult. Only a month has passed since I left his mother.

 Academy

I THOUGHT OF the weeks as junior maître d' as a training period. I had made mistakes. I would improve. I would learn French inside out. I would ask the international guests more interesting questions. I had already seen the senselessness of typing quotations from books at the end of the menu. I had stopped trying to flirt with Parivash. Soon, I would buy a new suit.

Ahmoud, however, had seen enough, and he sacked me. In the letter of dismissal, he said that I 'had not carried out my duties in the way expected'. I was horrified. In my town, in my family, the worst thing that could ever be said about you was that you had not carried out your duties in the way expected. If my father had known that I'd been sacked, he would have blushed with shame. Better to be dismissed for theft, assault or indecent exposure than for falling down on the job.

I left the hotel after a final breakfast – Ahmoud insisted on the breakfast – and lugged my suitcase into town with tears running down my cheeks. I was struggling to put together a story that my father might accept. 'Dad, it seems I just wasn't cut out to be a maître d', French was a big problem, Dad – I couldn't really speak French all that well, and my suit wasn't the proper sort of suit.' And so on. Excuses. My father would see that I was just making excuses. He would say, 'You didn't want to get your little pink hands dirty.'

Without money, it was difficult to know what I could do. I couldn't sponge off Jo and Randall, who were busy establishing their own lives. I saw them now and again, and it was obvious that we were no longer all in the one boat. I booked into a cheap hotel and went out to find a job. Making my way along Boulevard Pahlevi, one line of work after another suggested itself, only to be dismissed. I couldn't be a baker, for example. I couldn't start up a small restaurant. Maybe I could get a job as a shop assistant on the basis of my experience in the Myer Emporium, but what about language? I could barely make myself understood in Farsi. I came to the office of Iran Insurance, and called in to see Houshang.

'Well, it's not surprising, is it?' he said, when I told him I'd been sacked. 'You are too young for such work. Also, you stopped paying attention to Parivash.'

'But you told me to!'

'No. I told you that you would not succeed. I didn't tell you to stop. You insulted her.'

'Is that why I was sacked?' I was suddenly dizzy with hope. My father would easily, *easily* accept me losing my job because I had refused to sleep with the manager's wife. I could tell him that the manager's wife was bad tempered or ugly, and he would say, 'Not to worry, not to worry,' and put it all down to the malice of a scorned woman.

'No,' said Houshang, 'Ahmoud intended to sack you after four weeks. As soon as he hired you, he knew that he was wrong. You looked foolish.'

He had a suggestion. I should go down to the Iran–America Society office and see if they needed teachers. 'Have you been to university in Australia?' he asked, in a way that suggested that the only acceptable answer would be 'Yes'.

'Yes,' I said.

'Good. Speak to Louis at the Iran–America Society.'

The Iran–America Society office was on Boulevard Pahlevi. I had only a vague idea of the business of the place. I found it was a goodwill society and that it ran an English-teaching academy. Louis was lounging with his feet on his desk and his tie loosened. He looked like a private eye. I gave my name and told him that Houshang had sent me.

'He's a cunt, isn't he,' Louis said genially. 'Ladies' man. I must be jealous. What can we do for you? Sit down first.'

'I want to teach.'

'Teach what?'

'English.'

'Suits me. What've you got? BA? You look a bit young.'

'BA,' I nodded. I knew what it was.

'Not a limey, are you? Australian? Something like that? What university? Doesn't matter. Gimme your passport.'

Louis studied my passport for a minute or more without betraying any surprise. The date of birth would have shown me to be one of the few Arts graduates of my age in the world.

'I can give you three classes. You take each class four times a week. You're taking over from Janey. Gone AWOL somewhere. You start tonight. Don't tell me that's too soon, okay? If you don't do it, I have to. It's not too soon, is it?'

'No.'

I had time to skim the textbook. I walked into a classroom on the second floor in which twenty students, all my age or older, sat in silence with their books on their laps. There were no desks. I felt a rush of power. I was to spend quite a number of my future years teaching kids of just this age, but never again with the authority that buoyed me up that day.

After the class (on prepositions, with reference to a chapter from *Tom Sawyer*) a number of the students gathered around me, smiling shyly.

'Mister Roberts, you trousers too small for you.'

'Mister Robert, Ostraya far very far!'

'I shake you hand, Mister Illman.'

'Beatle, Mister Robert! Music, Beatle!'

'My students,' I wrote to my father that night, 'are quite friendly. I am glad that I changed my career because the people were not so friendly as this at the hotel. Also, a woman there wanted me to do something I didn't wish to do.'

Louis proposed an advance on my salary, and I accepted. At the hotel where I'd put up, Reza the manager, a good-natured boy of eighteen who had been given this responsible position by his uncle, slapped me on the back when I told him that I was now working as a teacher. A vernacular news service as rapid as the Internet conveyed information all over town, and Reza, who spoke English, confessed that he'd known of my teaching job at the society before I'd told him. But he hadn't wished to spoil my pleasure in telling him. In Shirazi culture (as I would learn) it was considered vulgar to spoil someone's surprise. I was never able to gauge whether I had succeeded in telling Reza anything about my circumstances that was not already well known to him.

What pleased Reza about my job was the salary. I would now be able to pay my hotel bill. He had, he said, been troubled when I'd booked in. He knew I had no money. He may have been required to throw me out. Now he was happy. He paraded me before the group of friends and relatives hanging about in the hotel office. These little groups of the unemployed, the unemployable and the retired gathered all over Iran. At the heart of the group you'd find a single occupied individual, but even he was occupied in such a desultory way that the distinction was hardly noticeable. Worry beads were counted, cups of tea ordered from a café.

Anything at all will fire the interest of these masters of enforced leisure. With Reza translating, they asked me a series of questions about the distant land of Australia, and each reply was met with either polite nods or short rounds of applause, with the hand not holding the teacup or cigarette beating a light tattoo on the thigh. Inevitably, the highlight of my account was a report on the stature and leaping prowess of the kangaroo. The bi-cameral parliamentary system baffled them, but they were interested in the Queen. Reza could not translate the word 'stupid'; I had to provide approximates.

'Fool.'

'Fool?'

'Silly.'

'Zealy? What is zealy mean?'

'Mad.'

'Ho! Mad?'

He translated 'mad', to the delight of the audience. It was, I think, a close neighbour of a term they would have wished to apply to the Shah. The laughter had a guilty-gleeful sound to it. I wanted to show just how bold I could be, perhaps telling the audience that my Prime Minister was also mad, but Reza thought it best to change the subject. He called over Ali, the hotel dogsbody, a tiny, toothless man with floppy ears like oven mitts, and told me that Ali was now my servant. 'You give Mister Ali three toomans,' Reza whispered. Since I had the money, I immediately offered it. Ali's gestures of obeisance embarrassed me. But I could not resist telling my father in my next letter that I now had a servant. 'I treat him very well,' I wrote. 'I disagree with slavery.'

The green island was as far away as ever, but at least I was supporting myself with the sweat of my brow. Sitting on my bed in my narrow little room, I wrote to my father every other day. What I craved was some endorsement from him; some recognition that by collecting a pay envelope each week, I was shaping up as I should. I had been collecting a pay envelope each week since I left school, of course, but now I was doing it in a foreign land. I thought some special mention should be made of the fact.

But my father's replies, much less regular than my own messages, only made me sad: 'Dear Bobby, We received your letter and we are very glad that you are well. It has been raining for a fortnight here so I am not able to get on with relaying those pipes below the pumping station as I need dry weather as there is a lot of digging which is very hard in the rain when the trench keeps filling. Doug Cornish and I went down to the tailrace a couple of night ago and took four brown trout (largest three and a half pounds) which goes to show as I always said that the brown will bite in the rain but the rainbow will not. I didn't understand what you were saying about the Hotel. Bertie asked about you, you can get that job back when you return if you wish. Kendra asked me to say hello to you. I looked in the Atlas for Iran in the Mid. East, but it isn't there, as this is an old Atlas perhaps in your next letter you can say where it is, if possible. I had some contact with Arabs in the war and I can warn you to be careful in all your dealings as they are inclined to be very, very tricky and cunning…'

The sky was blue each day. The sun shone. The city offered a riot of the exotic. At the turn into the market, an aged man in a rag of a turban stuffed the heads of three snakes into his mouth and stood, arms outstretched, while the long bodies of the serpents twisted and lashed. A tribesman down from the hills suddenly commanded his legion of wives and kids to fall to their knees to honour an eagle circling above. A parade of zealots, showing the whites of their eyes, advanced through the bazaar in little bunny hops, the better to torture their feet with the sharp pebbles in their shoes. A group of gaudily dressed women who were said to be Gypsies danced a jig on Pahlevi with their hands cupping their breasts.

But my father's letters made the world and its variousness seem utterly beside the point, as if I would know life only by stirring offal in Bertie's copper. And it seemed I could put aside ideas of love, delight and desire as the husband of a jewelled princess, because Kendra Phillips from fourth form, with her genial freckles and raucous laugh and her three little bad-boy brothers, was the girl who had my number, knew the plain facts about me. Kendra had liked me. My embarrassment had puzzled her. She didn't see anything mystical or attractively tragic in me at all.

News from home and the sadness it set working was one cause of distress. The mullahs were another. They were busy about the city each day, turning a censorial gaze on hemlines, hairdos and the tardy piety of the merchants in the marketplace. Their glares did not cause the Shirazis much alarm, but when they glared at me I felt spooked. They scowled at my pointed shoes and long hair, and shouted at me and made broad, sweeping motions with their arms, which I took to mean, 'Get back to Gomorrah, kid!' With their brown robes, white turbans and identically barbered beards, it was impossible to tell them apart. I'd escape from one at the end of Pahlevi, and a half-hour later his look-alike would be sneering as I entered the Shiraz Jazz Café at the other end of town.

Houshang laughed when I told him. 'Silly people,' he said. 'Don't worry. They're harmless.' Waking one afternoon in the hotel's courtyard where I was sunbaking, I found a pair of them squatting silently beside me. Disgust and lust contended in their expressions. When Reza appeared he salaamed and smiled obsequiously for the mullahs, but turned an exasperated eye on me. The mullahs withdrew slowly, lips pursed and eyes glittering.

'Mister Robert, so bad!'

'Pardon?'

'This!' And Reza plucked at my red Speedos.

'I'm sunbaking.'

'No! No no no!'

'Not allowed?'

Reza glanced left and right before leaning close to whisper, 'These men cruel. Cruel? You understand?'

'Cruel?'

Reza mimicked a person wielding a whip. 'Bang! Bang bang!'

'Oh,' I said.

Reza rubbed his behind, then brought his hand to his mouth and blew on it – to show, I think, the heat and pain that would have been concentrated there after a dash of the lash.

'Okay,' I said, wiser now.

My students at the Iran–America Society made attempts to educate me. After class, a group of them would walk me along the streets, pausing every so often to make a point.

'Who is this, Mister Robert?' They were nodding towards a tall, thin young man strolling languidly near the bazaar.

'I don't know,' I said.

'Beheshti, taking your money.'

Shamshiri, a cheerful, bespectacled boy of sixteen who had established himself as the cleverest student in any of my classes, rubbed his hands together then cast what I understood to be imaginary dice onto the sidewalk.

'Hoo! Beheshti too smart!' said Nashi.

'Beheshti is looking for you,' said Shamshiri.

'For me? Why?'

'For all English persons, for Americans, for Peace Corps. Shiraz people never trust him. Foreign people trust him only.'

'Too smart, Beheshti!' Nashi said again, admiringly.

We crossed into the bazaar and found Beheshti settling down to a hookah in a café. My students greeted him gaily then nudged me forward.

'Hi,' I said, and Beheshti, smiling charmingly, extended a long, white, prehensile hand.

'Give Beheshti ten toomans, Mister Robert.'

I gave up the ten toomans, reluctantly. The instant the note touched Beheshti's fingers, it disappeared. He didn't palm it or manipulate it in any way. He simply made it vanish. My students hooted and slapped their thighs and crooned with amazement. I, too, expressed my surprise. But when I asked for the note back, my students looked at me blankly.

'Your toomans gone, Mister Robert. Beheshti too smart.'

'But I only gave it to him because you told me to!'

Shamshiri, ushering me out of the café, spoke of the experience as if it were a valuable lesson for me. It was impossible for me to tell whether I was the butt of a joke or the victim of my students' naivety. I would not have needed any warning regarding Beheshti. He looked to me exactly like the crook he was.

Next I was required to meet an oddity of a different sort – a man who was said to be the only atheist in Iran. His name had come up when I was chatting with my students. They had wanted to know if I was Jewish, and if I was not – that is, if I was a Christian – how come I didn't wear a little cross around my neck like every other Christian? I said, nonchalantly, that I was an atheist. It took half an hour to make clear what an atheist was. The students chortled gleefully, as if my stupidity, which had already provided them with so much delight, had just revealed a new and even more thrilling dimension. The idea that there was a god who was not Allah seemed to them complete nonsense, but tolerable nonsense, as if you'd declared yourself a member of the Flat Earth

Society. The earth was round, no question, but if you persisted in believing it flat, best of luck to you. But to deny the existence of any god at all was like saying that the earth was not round and not flat, and in fact didn't exist. A name was spoken. Pissing themselves, my students let me know that here, here in Shiraz, another such atheist dwelt, name of Hakemi, only fellow in Iran stricken in the same way as I was.

Hakemi was a spectacle-repairer, and worked in his house on the hill near the Parki Saadi. We marched across town to meet him. I was expecting someone witty and ironic, someone with his tongue in his cheek and the twinkle of a lively intelligence in his eye. Hakemi wasn't like that. He was bad-tempered, shrill and impatient. As near as I could tell, his opening message to my students was that they piss off. They took no notice. Then followed a shouting match, a real treat for my students but obviously trying to Hakemi. Eventually the matter at hand was broached. Here's our teacher, an atheist and an idiot like you, you silly old bastard, so what do you think about that? – or so I guessed the introduction was made, judging from gestures. Hakemi, who didn't wear glasses himself but obviously needed to, squinted at me with his beaky nose about an inch from my face. 'Jesus,' he said to me. 'No Jesus?'

Now, I didn't wish to deny the historical existence of Jesus. But translation would be a problem. So I replied, mildly, 'Jesus, yes, God, no.'

'Jesus yes, God no?'

'Yes.'

This response seemed, I think, a bit fishy to Hakemi. He stood with his lips pursed and his head cocked to one side, thinking.

'Jesus yes, God no?' he said again.

'Yep.'

'Hakemi,' he said, jabbing his finger into his chest, 'Mohammed no, Allah no.'

'Mohammed no, Allah no?' I said.

'Mohammed no, Allah no.'

Hakemi looked pleased with himself. He'd established a standard of unbelief that left me looking like a quibbler. But my students had obviously prepared themselves for a more interesting afternoon. Nashi stepped forward, and roused Hakemi all over again. I asked Emmilef to translate.

'Nashi tells Hakemi you are saying God is mad.'

'Me? I didn't say that!' But I knew where this nonsense had come from. When I'd told Reza at the hotel that Queen Elizabeth was mad, the comment had become known to all my students. Nashi had decided that what I'd said of the Queen could equally be considered my judgement on the god I claimed did not exist. 'I said the Queen is mad. Not God. I didn't say God is mad.'

Hakemi, however, had seen a way to get his teeth into the seat of my pants. I had been revealed as a mere casuist. He barked back something that sent the students into hysterics. Shamshiri was being encouraged by the others to translate, but he seemed reluctant.

'What'd he say?' I demanded.

Prodded, punched and cajoled by the others, Shamshiri finally came through.

'Hakemi is saying you are having no brains...' (and here Shamshiri touched his temple)... 'and no... this...' (pointing at his crotch).

'No balls?'

'Yes. Bollis. No bollis. I am sorry Hakemi is saying this to you, Mister Hillman.'

'Tell Hakemi,' I said, stung, 'that I've got plenty of balls. Tell him I say *no* Jesus, *no* God. *Nothing.* Okay?'

'No Jesus, no God?'

'Right.'

Shamshiri, shrugging, gave Hakemi my new position. Hakemi waved a hand at me dismissively, and said something that delighted the students all over again.

'Now Hakemi is saying you are same as a woman, Mister Hillman!'

'I am not!'

Nashi whispered something to Shamshiri, who then whispered it to me.

'Mister Hillman, say to Hakemi he is monkey face!'

I might have, but after a few seconds' reflection I decided it was beneath my dignity to go on with the argument. In any case, Nashi had started his own brawl with Hakemi and was shaping up to punch him. He had to be dragged out of the house by the other students, with Hakemi raining insults on him. I last glimpsed Hakemi standing in the doorway with his arms folded, looking triumphant.

The students also thought it imperative that I meet a friend of theirs in the National Police, a lieutenant named Rasheef. He was in uniform when I first met him. I did not require the warning they gave me about staying on the good side of such a man. Rasheef, in his early twenties, had the swagger of a schoolyard bully enhanced by his employment in the office of licensed thug. He was a friend of my older male students, boys of eighteen and nineteen, but how they had come to know him so well was never explained. Houshang's conjecture was that Rasheef had probably befriended them, rather than the other way around. They all came from well-to-do families, and he would have seen advantage in this.

We met at the home of Nashi's married older brother, Adeem. In a small courtyard behind tall mud-brick walls, dishes of food were served over a period of hours. I have come to enjoy the sort of food I was offered that day, but it was a hard ask for me, aged seventeen, to keep a smile on my face while washing down fare made from ingredients I had not heard of with a spirit that smelled like turpentine. A bottle of tomato sauce would have made the world of difference.

A tabor and a fiddle were fetched late in the afternoon. Adeem, a renowned singer, took the stage. I sat listening for an hour or more to what sounded to me like the human voice mimicking the sound of water running down a plughole. The students were blissed-out, but Rasheef became restless. He called for the fiddle, and clowned with it in the manner of a man known to introduce grave reprisals when an audience disappointed him. The students laughed like hyenas. Encouraged, Rasheef asked for his pistol and passed a riotous half-hour cocking the gun against our temples. There was more hilarity to come. He had some 'sex books' to show us, which turned out to be a couple of medical volumes. With a great deal of sniggering, Rasheef displayed coloured plates of the female genitalia.

The next day, my students drove home the lesson of that appalling afternoon: Rasheef, like Beheshti, was a bad man. Signatures of sincerity and insincerity change from culture to culture, of course, and I couldn't pick either in Iran. Houshang tried to explain to me that attempting to achieve two contradictory aims at the one time was a typically Persian thing to do. The boys, he said, were probably trying to show off their powerful buddy in the National Police, while at the same time warning me to watch out. He said that Rasheef, unlike the mullahs, was properly dangerous. If he shot me in the back of the head and left me in the hills, no one would report finding my body. But why would he want to shoot me in the back of the head? Who could be less harmless than me? 'He likes you,' Houshang said. 'He might ask you to do something for him. Perhaps you will say no. Then he doesn't like you.'

'Do what for him?'

'I don't know. The police are corrupt. Rasheef makes friends with foreigners. I don't know what he wants with them.'

As it turned out, Rasheef did have a task for me. One evening, after my last class for the day, Nashi nervously asked me to walk with him down to the National Police headquarters. The other students shrank back, shrugging and muttering. But I felt very little apprehension. I had done no wrong. And if Rasheef asked me to do something I didn't want to do, I would refuse, and maybe he would be surprised at my strength of character and decide not to shoot me. There was also my trump card. I was an Australian. We were a nation of people to whom things did not happen.

At the police station, Nashi, more jittery with every passing minute, spoke briefly with a burly constable, gesturing towards me as if I had tagged along unbidden. I gazed around at framed portraits of the Shah, which hung everywhere. Rasheef emerged from his office and welcomed me with a smile. He told Nashi to get lost.

Once in his office, Rasheef himself seemed to me to grow almost as nervous as Nashi. He pointed at an ancient musket mounted on the wall, then took it down and invited me to sight along the barrel. He showed me a curved sword and encouraged me to touch the blade. 'Shop?' he said. After a moment's puzzlement, I said, 'Sharp.'

'Sharp?'

'Sharp. Very sharp.'

'Very sharp?'

'Very sharp, yes.'

'Very sharp.'

Rasheef then stood on one foot and raised the polished boot on the other foot.

'Show,' he said, pointing at the boot. 'Show. Yes?'

'Boot,' I said.

'Bood?'

'Boo – t. Boot.'

'Boot. Not show? Boot?'

I pointed to my own Beatle shoes. 'Shoe,' I said. Then, pointing to Rasheef's footwear, I said, 'Boot.'

Rasheef shot me a suspicious glance. Then understanding dawned. 'Ah!' he said, throwing his hands up to the ceiling. 'Show, little, boot – big!' he looked at me for confirmation.

'Shoe, little,' I said. 'Boot, big!'

He was delighted. He clapped his hands together and chuckled.

Serious once more, Rasheef stood before me and put his hands on my shoulders. Enunciating each word so carefully that his moustache was drawn up, then down, then stretched from side to side, he said, 'You... teaching... Rasheef... the English. Hokay?'

'Sure!'

He gazed at me in that unreliably sentimental way common in brutal men, spicks and specks of comradely love gathered up and held briefly in a misty film.

'Good!' he said. 'Very good!'

No sooner was I back on the boulevard than Nashi jumped out from behind a tree.

'Ho! Mister Robert! Mister Rasheef no hurting you!'

'Of course not!' I said.

As I made my triumphal way down Pahlevi, more and more of my students appeared from the shadows. Shamshiri, looking sheepish, was the first to ask the reason for the summons from Rasheef.

'He wants me to teach him English,' I said.

'Mister Rasheef will pay you excellent?' he asked.

This question reminded me that payment hadn't been discussed. Something about Rasheef's manner, as I reflected on it, made me think that money was probably not part of the deal. The mullahs lost interest in me. Rasheef became my pal after a half-dozen vile English lessons during which he mastered the names of all the female body parts.

Without distractions, my craving for love resurfaced. I'd given up tagging along with Houshang on his visits to

Persepolis. The sight of so many classy women stumbling back after a tryst behind a pillar with Houshang was souring my belief in the transfiguring power of love. Sex for these women seemed nothing more than a holiday activity. Then one afternoon in my Upper B class, Shayda Ashadi smiled at me. Shayda was pure poetry – dark-eyed, blushful, heartbreakingly pretty. Also very intelligent. She had written an essay on birds that concluded with the line, 'A bird is like our heart.' That line by itself had torn a huge hole in my guts, but the smile was the real killer. I thought, Oh God, she loves me!

Wasting no time, I wrote her a letter asking her to meet me in the library after my last class. I handed her the letter as she was leaving. It was the birthday of the Persian poet Saadi, and that seemed propitious. My last class passed in a blur. Dear God, I prayed silently, if you let me have Shayda Ashadi, I will gladly die a painful death at your convenience – after a couple of years with her, say. Or if that's too much to ask, a couple of months. I waited in the library for Shayda. I barely breathed. My heart had stopped beating altogether.

Shamshiri wandered in wearing an embarrassed smile. He had the letter I'd written to Shayda in his hand.

'Is Shayda coming?' I asked, knowing that she would not come, couldn't come, had been forbidden to come, had fallen into the hands of the mullahs, perhaps had even killed herself.

'Mister Hillman…' Shamshiri began.

'Yes?'

'Mister Hillman…'

'She's not coming, is she?'

Shamshiri lifted his hands, shook his head. He gave me the letter.

'Mister Hillman, this is not possible in Iran. This is not possible. She is very sorry.'

I slumped back to the hotel like a zombie. Honouring the tradition of the broken-hearted in the hour of grievous loss, I cried myself into a stupor and considered dashing my brains out against a hard surface.

Late in the evening, Houshang pushed open the door to my room. He stood staring at me with his arms folded across his chest.

'Louis called me on the telephone,' he said. 'He would have come himself, but he was afraid he would kill you.'

'He can kill me if he likes,' I said.

Houshang looked up at the ceiling and sighed. I was sitting hunched on the side of my bed in my Speedos. My proper underpants were drying on the line in the courtyard.

'My poor dear friend,' said Houshang, lowering himself onto the one available chair after removing my garments from it with an expression of distaste, 'why have you insulted Miss Ashadi in this way? After all I have told you? Do you know who she is? Of course you don't. Her father is very wealthy. He is very sophisticated. Otherwise he would have had you beaten very badly. But you have broken his heart. Have I not told you that no Iranian girl will go out with a foreigner unless she has lost her virginity? You have called her a prostitute by asking her to come with you. It is a bad insult to her, and much worse to her father and to her mother. She will never come to your class again. No Iranian girl will come to your class again.'

'I love her,' I said.

'Then why did you insult her?'

'I only wanted to tell her how I felt.'

'Fortunately,' said Houshang, ignoring what I considered the most important issue, 'you are very young. Mister Ashadi has taken this into account. But you must write a letter of apology. I will tell you what to say.'

And he did. I sat at my typewriter and took dictation. Whenever I objected to the phrasing – I would never myself say, for example, 'Much foolishness is to be found in the young' – Houshang struck me on the back of the head with his hand. When we were done, he took the letter, folded it neatly, and told me to walk along Pahlevi with my eyes averted twice a day for the next week to show my contrition. I told him I would do no such thing, but he knew me well enough to feel confident that I would.

He was right about the girls abandoning my classes. The next day, Louis showed me a list of almost forty names – all girls who had withdrawn. They had been placed in other classes. Louis, who took the view that the whole disaster had been about sex, asked me why I didn't just bang the Peace Corps girls. 'That's what they're here for, Mister! Get wise!'

My students – the boys – also took the view that the whole business was about sex. Not long after the Saadi's Birthday Massacre, they invited me to a party. These 'parties' (I had been to a couple) were fairly severe trials of your goodwill, unless you were Iranian. Nothing happened rapidly. About an hour before the food was ready, you were invited to sit down and eat. After eating, you sat just where you were for a further hour, singing the praises of your host. As an honoured guest, a singer and a man with a peculiar twanging instrument may sit before you performing some old Persian saga of love and woe, the singer driving you nuts with his exaggerated gestures. All the while, your host is whispering a translation of the saga into your ear: 'Now come Ali. Very unhappy, he, not liking for his sister to marrying this man, very bad man, face ugly like monkey... Ho! – Ali kill him! Ali cut off his head! Ha!' I accepted the invitation, taking it as part of my penance.

But it was a different sort of party that my students had in mind. Their delicacy had prevented them spelling it out. They took me in a taxi to an area out along the airport road where the city's prostitutes gathered. This location (I came to know this later) palliated the sensibilities of the city fathers. They argued that since only immoral foreigners and maybe a few vile Arabs would want to associate with prostitutes, business could be transacted on the way to the airport, before the disgusting clientele flew away to somewhere else. But the truth was that the wealthy Arabs and immoral foreigners preferred the classier women found in the city itself; the airport road prostitutes served the ordinary Shirazis, on the cold, hard ground beside the highway.

We were six in the taxi. My students, as good Muslims, didn't drink alcohol, but it was no sin to pour Raki down the throat of a Christian. I was drunk by the time the taxi pulled up at a barren area where moonscape desert peaks stood silhouetted against the night. Three or four other taxis were already parked. The rollicking students – high on 7 Up – struggled to push their heads out the windows, calling lewdly to dark, immobile shapes covered head to foot in burkas. Two of the shapes eventually responded. After a few minutes' harsh bargaining, the women clambered into the taxi. They quickly mastered the boys with slaps and oaths, then showed their faces to me. It was impossible to see much in the darkness of the taxi, but the driver fetched a torch from the glovebox and shone its beam onto each face. One of the women had perhaps already celebrated a fortieth or even a fiftieth birthday. The other was young and pretty. I attempted to kiss both of them but only succeeded in getting my ears boxed. 'These ladies don't want kissing,' Shamshiri whispered to me. The older woman made a long angry speech as the taxi took off, gesturing towards me with an open hand. Shamshiri was obliged to tell me once more, 'You must not kiss these ladies, Mister Hillman.'

We arrived at last at an orchard (so it was explained to me), surrounded by mud-brick walls as high and imposing as those of a fortress. One of the students, Mashid, was the son of the owner of the orchard. Mashid jumped out of the taxi and shouted at the ancient wooden gate that barred our entrance. A voice responded, and the gates were slowly eased open by an old man dressed in rags and patches. Mashid and the old man bickered in the taxi's headlights, the argument becoming more and more animated. Finally, the old man hobbled over to the taxi and thrust his head in through the window. He studied me sceptically, making clucking noises with his tongue.

The old man's objections apparently overcome, we bundled out of the taxi and headed into the orchard. The dark bodies of trees stretched away downhill. A night wind in the boughs filled the air with a sound like waves breaking on a beach. Around a gurgling fountain, the students parleyed with the women over money. Mashid kept throwing up his hands and walking away from the negotiations, only to return with ever-more heated complaints. Shamshiri, maintaining a scholar's disinterested manner, wandered over to me to ask mildly if I required only one or both of the women. I said, 'Both.' Shamshiri returned to the parley, conveyed my message, and a sudden silence replaced the haggling. All eyes were turned to me. Then the students began to applaud and laugh.

'Ho, Mister Illman! Ho ho, Hrobbat!'

The conference resumed, with more shouting than ever.

'One,' said Shamshiri, approaching me again. 'For two, most expensive.'

'Okay, one,' I said.

'Which one you like best, Mister Hillman?'

The two women stood glaring at me – the pretty one and the one old enough to be her mother. I wanted the one who was young and pretty, but did not wish to hurt the feelings of the older one. So I chose the mama, to the surprise of everyone.

A shed was found for us, the floor covered in rotting apples. The mama hoisted her burka, lay down on the apples and signalled for me to make haste. I made what haste I could, but the Raki had numbed my body and all I could think of was getting back to the hotel and going to sleep. The mama hissed angrily in my ear as I laboured away. My students gathered around and shouted exhortations. At last I was done, and the mama heaved me aside and raced to the fountain to wash herself, trailing a string of curses.

Once we had returned the women to the airport road, Shamshiri felt at liberty to disclose that Shayda's father had paid for the evening's fun.

'That was nice of him,' I said.

'Now he will tell Shayda that you do this sex with these ladies,' Shamshiri added.

'What? Why!'

'Shayda will be thinking you are a very bad man.'

All of the students seemed satisfied with this outcome. They encouraged me to accept the wisdom of the arrangement, patting my back and hugging me. I was mortified and the next day hurried to hear Houshang's opinion.

'No, I don't think so,' he said, when I asked him if Shayda's father had paid for the prostitutes. 'But maybe.'

'To make Shayda think I'm bad?'

'Perhaps.'

'Why does he want her to think I'm bad?'

'Miss Ashadi was very upset.'

'Because I wrote her that letter?'

'She is a little bit modern. Perhaps she likes you.'

'Oh, God!'

'It's better,' Houshang went on in his languid way. 'She will go to the university in Tehran. She is going to study sea creatures. She is a modern young woman. We need many modern young women in Iran.'

Heartbreak is awful, but at least it gives you a reason for living. I went about as a rejected suitor for a month or more. Much of the time, I was in tears. I re-read *A Farewell to Arms* and relished the final scenes where Catherine loses her life in the hospital. It was a solace to have something in common with Lieutenant Henry. I had loved, I had paid.

With increasing distaste I carried on with Rasheef's English lessons. The illustrations in the medical books so dominated them that I couldn't help feeling that he had no interest in

English except as a medium of pornography. I'd been required to write out every colloquial term for the male and female genitalia that I could think of. 'This is the dick of a man... This is the cock of a man... This is the tool of a man...' Rasheef would sit at his desk, huddled over the sheet of paper on which I'd written these obsessive messages, struggling to get his lips and moustache around the words. It was not very inspiring work, even allowing for the mild thrill I felt when Rasheef came to a term I'd made up: 'This is the miggy moggy of a man... This is the winny wunny of a woman...'

But it was the thug in Rasheef that properly distressed me. I was in his office with him one afternoon, working on the list, when a subordinate barged in, shoving a boy of about twelve before him. The boy stood cowering, head hanging low, while Rasheef and his underling muttered together. Without warning, Rasheef belted the boy on the side of the head, knocking him across the room. I half came to my feet, but was motioned to sit down. The boy trembled over to Rasheef again, and was again belted. The malice that Rasheef radiated kept me in my seat, my legs gone to jelly. He hit the boy about six times, each blow as heavy as the last. Nobody spoke a word. When the boy was taken away, Rasheef looked at me and made a strange face – he seemed to be imitating a sad clown, mouth turned down. I realised that he was imitating me. He sent me on my way with a pitying look – reminding me to return the next day.

My failure to stand up for the boy who'd been beaten so cruelly made it impossible for me to approach Rasheef when my work visa ran out. Performing a service for him was one thing; asking for his help was more than my stomach could cope with. I decided that I would simply leave Iran. I would make my way to Pakistan, to India, to Ceylon. My old Ceylon plan was still intact: make some money as a journalist, take a boat to Mombasa, another boat to the Seychelles, locate the gentle, bare-breasted women of those islands, relax in the warmth of their love forever. I noticed that I no longer endowed the Seychelles women with anything hectic in the way of libido. It would be enough if they simply cradled my head on their cushiony breasts, whisked away flies, stroked my cheeks with gull feathers. And yet even as I conjured this tender vision, I had ceased to believe in it. Now, I merely yearned for it to exist.

With my suitcase packed and my green suit freshly pressed, I made the rounds of my friends. Randall, thriving now at the hospital, where even the surgeons deferred to him in moments of crisis, listened to my plans with a frown.

'I was beginning to think you'd got some brains,' he said. 'You'll get slaughtered.'

'I'll be fine.'

'No, kid, you'll get slaughtered.'

Jo, studying me without much interest from behind the reception desk at the British Council, told me that if I had attempted to leave Shiraz without having repaid her all that I owed her, she would have had me forcibly detained. Since I had repaid her, there seemed little point in the telling.

'You should go back to Australia and finish school,' she said.

'I don't want to.'

'Your parents should jolly well have you fetched back! Honestly, children like you running loose in a place such as this!'

I attempted to kiss her on the cheek, but she yelped and punched me. Then her self-righteous anger disappeared. Her shoulders drooped and her eyes went silver with tears. 'Honestly, Robert. Listen to me. None of us should be here. It's foolish. It's not an adventure, it's simply foolish. One hates to admit it. But there it is and here we are. Go home and be sensible. Please.' She gave me one of the egg and pickle sandwiches from her lunchbag to take with me.

Houshang, on hearing my news, went straight into sage mode. 'A journey east or west is taken in one's own company. Robert in Pakistan remains Robert. We are together with ourselves forever.'

'Thanks for everything, Houshang.'

'You should remain here. Perhaps you could make a marriage with Miss Ashadi.'

'You told me she was going to Tehran to study sea creatures!'

'Who knows? Indeed, who knows?'

'I'm not even a Muslim.'

'Yes, that would be a great difficulty. Besides, her father would punish you severely if you approached her.'

'Goodbye, then.'

'Goodbye my dear friend.'

WE'RE FISHING IN the tailrace. I'm using a heavy sinker to keep my bait on the bottom in the turbulent water that spews from the powerhouse, but my father hardly bothers with a sinker. It's his theory that trout are canny enough to regard a stationary worm in a powerful current as suspicious. He believes that you should think like a trout to catch a trout, and there must be something in what he says because he has three fish, rainbows, while I have none.

It's February, and very hot. The tiny, darting lizards that live along the bank keep to the shadows of the rocks. The ravens in the wattles take awkward leaps to reach branches that are out of the sun. It's too hot for fishing, as far as I'm concerned, but my father is in a good mood and insists on me being with him. I suit him perfectly when he's in a good mood. He likes to talk, I'm happy to listen.

This is Saturday. On Friday, Dad won five pounds in Tatts. The five pounds will help with things a bit, but it means much more to him than that. He had never before won so much as ten shillings in Tatts, despite buying a ticket every week for twenty years. The win means his luck is turning. More good fortune will follow. I'm happy for him, too, but I can't help thinking that five pounds doesn't represent much of a return for the hundreds of pounds he's spent on tickets up to now. I wouldn't dream of pointing that out, though. When you live in the care of unhappy and disappointed parents, episodes of optimism mean the world to you. You begin to believe, along with your parents, that things are going to change. But you remain wary, even as you smile.

One thing I enjoy about my Dad is that he doesn't lecture me when we're out fishing. I don't have the knack that Dad has. My line tangles;

I cast into snags; I don't know the signs and I don't know how to land a trout even when I hook one. But Dad recognises that I will likely never improve (he's tried to help, he's been a model of patience), and leaves me alone.

Dad never initiates the stories of the green island that I so relish hearing. There's a protocol. I ask him a question about the war, and little by little we get to the green island. So, on this burning Saturday, I ask the question. The question can't just come from nowhere. It has to be related to whatever's going on. Dad might be browsing through the Australasian Post, for example, and I might ask if the women of the green island were as beautiful as the woman in a bathing suit on the magazine's cover. And he would snort, as if such a comparison were too ludicrous to take seriously, then tell me why a beautiful white girl can never match a beautiful black girl, not ever. Today, I use the weather. I ask him if it was as hot on the green island as it is here, and is that why those women went about naked. Nope, he says, it was hot but not all that hot. Where it was hot, he says, was Palestine. I have a feeling right away that stories of Palestine are not going to include much in the way of naked women.

But Palestine it is. It appears that Dad, in common with a great many other Australian soldiers, was first sent to the Middle East before being rushed back home to fight the Japs. I hear about the desert, and I'm told that you don't know what heat is until you've stood on parade with the sun baking the back of your neck and the heat of the sand coming right through the soles of your boots. Yep, that was Palestine. That was the Middle East. It can be quite beautiful, too, but Jeez, you wouldn't want to live there.

What I realise later is that Dad doesn't talk about the green island when he's happy. And that's why I so rarely hear him talk about the desert.

 Desert

AS I HITCHED up to Tehran, my heart in my boots, I was overcome by an intense bout of self-consciousness. It was like reading a novel and suddenly being visited by a vision of the writer in his under-junders with a fag in his mouth and a bottle of cheap red wine close by. You see the writer picking his nose; you see his scrotum peeking out of his jocks; you see his crowing self-congratulation when he mints a fancy sentence. What I saw was the idiot I had mostly managed to keep concealed from myself. I saw the story of my quest as just plain nuts. I saw the anxious expressions of a host of people gazing at a gangly child who should have locked been up for his own protection, as Jo had suggested. I saw the soft, pleading look in my own eyes, the sort of look that appears on the face of a dog that has taught itself to make a living out of apology. Narrating my story as I went along, fashioning its scenes, I was all at once hobbled by an inability to suspend disbelief. How can a man with an exposed scrotum and a finger in his nostril expect me to take anything he writes seriously? Or the life I was narrating for myself – what confidence could

I possibly have in a child who imagined the things that I had imagined?

The truck driver who had picked me up stopped for the night at an outdoor hotel, Garden of Heaven, just north of Isfahan. Hotels like this are found all over the Middle East. You pay for a small wooden bed, carry it out to a vast courtyard and set it up wherever you can find a space. In the Garden of Heaven that night, forty or fifty beds stood scattered across the courtyard. The juddering snores of a neighbour kept me awake. When he woke, he raised himself on his side and stared at me, at first with suspicion and then with smiling curiosity. 'Chakar?' he said, meaning 'Explain this'. 'Australia,' I said, and he nodded without understanding and went back to sleep. I listened to an old man chanting prayers with such exaggerated gestures of piety that his neighbours giggled and winked at each other. A mother whispered to her children, huddled close to her beneath a snowy white sheet. Four men sat cross-legged on their beds, absorbed in a game of what appeared to be euchre, the dealer flighting the cards expertly through the air.

I stared at the stars and recited 'The Man From Snowy River' to keep my fear at bay. My father had encouraged me to learn the poem by heart when I was ten. I remembered tears running down through the stubble on his cheeks when he first read it to me. It was the triumph of the boy whom Old Harrison had doubted that moved him. He liked to believe, even as an adult, that he would one day confound the Old Harrisons of his own life, all of those who'd doubted him.

I never knew why he thought he was doubted. People admired him. They thought him a reliable worker, a good enough father, a wonderful fisherman, a decent bloke. Sometimes, though, when he was drunk or almost, he would whisper to me if we were alone that he had done things he was ashamed of. 'Can't pretend I haven't, Bobby. Get dark on myself at times.' I thought he'd maybe done some cruel things in the war, but looking at it that night under the stars, I concluded that he'd never done bad things, but wished he could hold it against himself that he'd been wicked. I wished for wickedness myself, but a stylish wickedness of the sort that didn't make you feel awful. I might say to some woman, 'My dear, I'm a bad lot.'

'But his hardy mountain pony he could scarcely raise a trot,' I whispered, with my hands over my ears to dull the warbling of the old man's prayers, 'He was blood from hip to shoulder from the spur…' How could I make myself vivid? Break into life? I could hear Bertie summing me up when I returned to the butcher's shop: 'Had your fun? Want you to wake up a bit if you're going to do this proper. Remember those fuckin' sausages you used to make? Looked like bedsocks filled with rags…'

Around me, the settling sounds of the other guests were diminishing. The old man had rolled up his prayer rug. The gamblers had packed it in. I heard only the roar of the trucks on the highway, the clink of the tea glasses being washed, the crying of children cut off by the soft shushing of a mother. 'So Clancy rode to wheel them – he was racing on the wing Where the best and boldest riders take their place, And he raced his stock-horse past them, and he made the ranges ring With the stockwhip as he met them face to face…'

Isfahan at five in the afternoon was dark and wet. A motionless grey sky stretched from horizon to horizon, and the rain fell soundlessly. I found a hotel in the centre of the city, then went in search of a second-hand bookshop I recalled from my first visit nine months earlier. Why it should be so I don't know, but I could always find English-language bookshops in the Middle East. I had sought it out not because I was short of reading material, but for its comfort. I ignored the shelves at the front of the shop that were dedicated to travel guides and picture books, and settled out of sight amongst the novels. I was immediately at peace. Tears filled my eyes as I welcomed the relief. I came across a novel by Jon Cleary and turned it about in my hands, thinking that Cleary, a fellow Australian, may once have been as stupid as I was. I searched avidly for more Australians. I found *They're A Weird Mob*, *The Summer of the Seventeenth Doll*, a collection of Australian verse, *The Tree of Man*, *Robbery Under Arms*, and a book of cartoons with the famous 'Stop laughing – this is serious' drawing by Stan Cross on the cover. I sat with this small pile of books on my lap, trying to think of something that I would always remember – perhaps, 'Oh yes, my great passion for Rolf Boldrewood began in Iran, strange as it may seem.' But I didn't feel attracted to *Robbery Under Arms*. In the end I purchased the book of cartoons (I still own it) and *The Spy Who Came in From the Cold*.

I finished reading *The Spy Who Came in From the Cold* early in the morning. I lay on my bed staring at the skylight with the book beside me. The big problem with learning anything about life from a book is that other people respond to you as if you were the same person as before you read the book. I wanted to announce that I now knew how deeply immoral were the intelligence services of countries all over the world. And how important love was. And loyalty. And what it means to stand up and say, 'You cynical bastards – I'm no longer your patsy,' as Leamas had. I felt tougher for having read the book. But the fact was that the manager was standing at the front door when I headed out for an early morning walk in the rain, obviously concerned that I would leave without paying my bill. And right there, I was up against it. I said I would pay when I left. He said, 'You pay now.' So I paid. If he'd known what had happened inside me, he might have thought that it was dangerous to insult me. But he didn't know. Instead of being out in the rain looking at life through fresh eyes, I was out in the rain feeling hurt. And I remained hurt. Oh God, just to be *commanding* – even for an hour!

I walked for a long time, the rain too warm to create much discomfort. The sight of me wandering the narrow streets in my green suit and tie must have puzzled the Isfahanis, but they didn't show it. I was in a maze of narrow lanes with broad gutters running down the centre. Doors opened onto courtyards, and here and there I glimpsed people, poor people rousing themselves for the day's work, the men unshaven, the women seeming always alert and versatile in a homely way. I saw one mother managing to keep a black umbrella aloft while washing a child's face at an ancient courtyard fountain, tending a naked baby in her lap and tickling the tummy of a blissed-out puppy with her toe. Groups of children with intent faces hurried down the lanes to school, books wrapped in plastic shopping bags to shield them from the rain. People shouted all the time, even if only a short distance apart, but it was not angry shouting. Carts and tiny three-wheeled vans bounced along the lanes, barely avoiding the centre gutter. One cart, pulled by what looked like a cross between a German Shepherd and a goat, displayed a picture of a huge white tooth, and I could only think the tiny, stooped man at the reins must be a roving dentist. Another man, a knife sharpener, carried a grindstone on his back; files of various grades hung on long cords from his belt.

Amongst all these tradesmen, mothers and hurrying schoolchildren, I felt the burden of my idleness and fretted for proper employment. It occurs to me now that both the burdens I carried around the world – the need to keep my little pink hands from staying too clean; the need to make it big with dusky women – were strapped across my shoulders by my father. He could have made things a lot easier for me if he'd just taken the time to say, 'Best thing, have fun.'

I headed south-east from Isfahan on the long journey to the Pakistan border. The heat in the parched mountains and the desert forced me to surrender the advantage of hitching in my green suit. It was my belief that the truck drivers thought me too well got-up to be left on the roadside, but the real reason that I was offered rides so readily was, I am sure, the simple goodwill of the drivers. Refusing to give up the last vestiges of sophistication, I kept my tie on. When it became so hot that I couldn't bear a tight collar, I at least tried to show by my demeanour that I was a person who would *normally* hitch across the desert in a suit and tie.

I had no money. My strategy for survival was barter. The rides were free, but the food was not. In scores of tiny eateries along the dirt highway to Yazd, to Rafsanjan, to Kerman, I gave up items of clothing in exchange for a bowl of beans and a plate of watery yoghurt. The less-fancy shirts went first, then my Speedos, my T-shirts, a pair of Dunlop runners, my spare belt, two of my three ties. My primitive method of payment didn't seem to raise any eyebrows. It was the desert; trucks, glass windows and bottles were about the only things that hadn't been around when Mohammed was a boy. Occasionally I flourished. I had a coup in Kerman, when from the lucky-dip of my suitcase I pulled out a box of condoms purchased twelve months earlier from a pharmacy in Little Collins Street. I'd bought them on the advice of old Vince in the ladies' shoe department at the Myer Emporium. 'You'll want some frangers,' he'd told me. 'And first couple of times you go out with a sheila, pay for her tucker.' The Kermanis knew immediately what the condoms were, and cackled with delight as if news of them would bring the desert girls bounding down from the hills. I ate royally and was allowed to sleep on the restaurant floor for the night.

Finding a bed on other occasions was difficult. The outdoor hotel people were a little less patient with barter. Perhaps the lack of a concrete exchange bothered them. A bowl of beans for a shirt was obviously a deal, but what value did you put on sleep? I slept on roadsides, in cemeteries (a popular kipping place for the homeless of south-eastern Iran), in trucks, under trucks and sometimes, gratefully, on the beds of pitying samaritans.

In Iran, the deeper you travel into the sticks, the more familiar you become with donkeys. (I wonder if the donkey's role in the development of human community has ever been thoroughly investigated.) In the tiny, arid towns of the Kerman

Desert, often the only thing getting along under its own steam is a donkey, with a boy and a haystack swaying on its back. I saw one poor beast barely able to put hoof before hoof under the burden of an automobile engine carried on a platform strapped to its shoulders and rump. I thought of the little haulier I'd seen die in Istanbul, who must have lived his life as a donkey. I pitied the poor beasts, but slung myself and my bulky suitcase onto their backs whenever a ride was offered.

Plodding along with a grinning boy holding the rope bridle of the donkey, the desert like rusted iron running away to hills baked black and red, I never for a second felt that I was anything other than a tourist. My thoughts penetrated far enough into the lives of the people around me to register if they were rich or poor or very poor, and no further. I was an Australian on an adventure – ill-conceived though it was. The world and all its landscapes existed for me to dawdle through. The people of the world existed to play implausible roles in one-dimensional dramas of my own concoction. Extraordinary that the ego of even a very dim child should function as such a tough carapace!

And yet, perhaps my limitations made me a more honest tourist. At least I wasn't scurrying from site to site collecting insights. And I wasn't searching for a culture to adopt. Some of the great travellers – both D. H. and T. E. Lawrence, for example – were searching for a hidey-hole in cultures they had no part in creating, prepared to daub their white skins with colours that would blend in. For all the ludicrousness of my quest, it did maintain a Lord Jim, nut-case candour. I was a simple white boy craving escape and glory. It never occurred to me, or to Jim, to give up our green suits and adopt the gorgeous garb of the natives.

It was cold at night in the desert; I had to suit-up before settling down. The jacket of the green suit began to look shabby so, rather than watch it lose all its allure, I swapped it in Kerman for a bowl of bean paste. The paste was certainly food, but it didn't taste like food and I bitterly regretted making the deal. It was now impossible for me to let the natives know how sophisticated I could look if I wanted to.

It was probably to compensate for my outward appearance that I started reading some of the non-fiction works I'd picked up in the hostel in Athens. I lurched through *Eros and Civilization* without making the slightest sense of it. In any case, there was nobody to impress with my choice of literature. A truck driver noticed the naked woman on the cover and took it for a dirty book; when I showed him that there were no other pictures, he lost interest. Equally unlikely to impress was a dictionary of literary terms that I peered into. I made it my task to memorise terms that I thought might come in handy one day, such as *ipse dixit* and *leitmotiv*. I was also taken with the illustration of meiosis from a Housman poem, and quoted it aloud for weeks: 'Long for me the rick will wait, And long will wait the fold, And long will stand the empty plate, And dinner will be cold.' The lines kept company in my head with 'The Man From Snowy River', my other memorised piece. *Fowler's Modern English Usage* was impossible then to enjoy. But I laboured to grasp the distinction in the use of 'will' and 'shall', and more or less mastered it. The knowledge allowed me to so contrive a letter to my father and sister that every 'will' became a 'shall'. Fortunately, I had no money to post it.

I did find myself enjoying E. P. Thompson's *The Making of the English Working Class*, however. I hadn't expected to. But it was thrilling, and just as *The Spy Who Came in From the Cold* ensured that I understood everything about international politics, so *The Making of the English Working Class* convinced me that I understood everything about everything.

The derelict look crept up on me. It wasn't just the dirty clothes; it was the broken fingernails and the zip of my fly held shut with a safety pin. By the time I reached Bam, west of the Pakistan border, I was filthy. I sold my typewriter, and with the loot gave myself a wash, had the zip on the trousers of my green suit replaced, fed myself, and rented a bed in an outdoor hotel in the shadow of a mosque. I enjoyed feeling clean for a time, but remorse overwhelmed me. After a poor night's sleep I hurried back to the tinsmith who'd bought my Olivetti, prepared to offer the remainder of my wardrobe in exchange for it. The Latin alphabet was of no use to him, after all.

He had the typewriter displayed amongst his traditional stuff – trays, dishes, bowls, ewers. I suppose it was meant to attract the curious. He declined my wardrobe with an expression of sorrow, a hand on his heart, head bowed. Merchants and shoppers gathered around, some seeming to take my side in the dispute. In my desperation I'd arranged all my clothes in a row – spare trousers, two shirts, green cardigan, last tie, spare belt, socks, singlets, underpants. I added half of my books, a used tube of toothpaste, a pair of thongs and two biros. Nothing doing.

My chief advocate, a greengrocer who'd wandered over from his stall, cast his hand along the row of garments, calling passionately for the tinsmith to get sane (as I guessed). He held up a book in each hand, shaking them at the heavens, as if he were asking God himself to witness the perversity of a tinsmith who would not yield up an Olivetti he couldn't use in exchange for a full Western wardrobe with a veritable library thrown in. Nothing doing, still. My advocate gave up the case with a shrug that said 'Tinsmiths, waste of space', gave me a hug of commiseration and went back to his vegies. I packed everything back into my suitcase and slouched away. I felt sick. Without my Olivetti, I was just a kid wandering around the Middle East. A true writer or journalist or reporter would not have sold his typewriter, no matter how filthy he was.

Too upset to battle my way across the desert on donkeys and trucks, I spent the last of the Olivetti money on a bus fare to Zahedan, right on the Pakistan border. The bus set off in the cool of the evening, feeling its way over the rough surface of the desert road and leaving the road behind altogether whenever a slightly less dangerous route offered itself. I had a seat at the back of the bus. For the first quarter-hour of the journey, all the children sat turned around in their seats, facing me. Craving a little endorsement, I tried to look as interesting as their curiosity suggested I might be. I smiled, wiggled my eyebrows up and down, made funny faces. The kids gave me up as a dead loss. When night fell, I settled sulkily back in my seat and thought of Miss Ashadi, and of how little allowance the Iranians made for romance and of how happy I might have been with Miss Ashadi if only vile religion hadn't played havoc with our stars.

On the broad back seat of the bus, two men cleared a little space and played chess, skilfully replacing the pieces whenever the lurching bus threw the board about. The bus was unlit, so the game was played by the flame of a cigarette lighter. One player seemed anxious, and kept peering out into the blackness. For what? I wondered. What did he expect to see? Iran seemed to me more than ever a truly joyless, wowser-ish country where people nursed their sorrows. The tiny specks of light that showed out in the desert night I took to be the fires of people futilely clinging to a life of sinew and bone in the arid wastes. What was the *point* of Iran? People didn't even read books, except for prayer books. The children only had to glance at their parents and their whole lives were revealed to them: a burka and babies for the girls; poverty and endless prayer for the boys, with maybe a game of chess to relieve the monotony.

My irritation with the anxious chess player mounted, as he took on the whole burden of my disappointment with life. I hated his stupid unshaven face, and the dog-like vacancy in his black eyes. And then, without warning, he came to life, quickly forfeited this fifth or sixth game, and bustled with a small bundle down the aisle to the front of the bus. Ahead, a light shone, a swaying light. The bus ground to a stop and the man jumped down, followed by shouts of farewell from the other passengers. A woman was waiting for him, a woman with a lantern. In its glow, her face shone with joy. The man threw his arms around her and stroked her hair, which she had left revealed. The passengers crowded to wave to him from the windows, and both he and the woman waved back. The bus fired up and heaved itself onto the road. I felt

206

ashamed. As compensation, I agreed to play chess with the man's companion. I enjoyed the games more and more, and was still playing when the bus pulled into Zahedan.

For no reason I could name, I expected to be more appreciated in Pakistan than I had been in Iran, or anywhere else for that matter. My sense of hope, like that of most children, was not flinty; it was more like putty – capable of being flattened without ever quite losing its elasticity. The sound of a country's name was enough to make me feel that things were about to change for the better. Pakistan. Pak Ee Stan. Surely there was magic in the name of that ancient land. (I did not know that Pakistan had not existed until 1948.) I would see things I had never seen before. These things would act on me in ways that I couldn't even guess at. Enchanting, perfumed valleys full of nightingales and cinnamon trees awaited me. Places that the rest of the world hardly knew about would welcome me. Amazing qualities of my own would suddenly flourish in this new climate. Pakistan would be exactly, precisely where I was meant to be.

All this I believed. At the same time, I knew that it was probably nonsense. But I had a high tolerance of nonsense.

WHEN RONALD RYAN is condemned to death by hanging in 1967, my father tells me that the bastard is only getting what he deserves. I haven't asked Dad what he thinks about the hanging, but he tells me anyway. With all the hoopla in the newspapers, I have gradually become aware that Ronald Ryan will be hanged on a certain day and at a certain time, and that I and everyone else will know that date and time in advance. This is a terrible piece of knowledge.

Dad is hectic about the hanging. He's worried that the public outcry might prevent it going ahead. He doesn't want Ronald Ryan to spend his life on free bed-and-board in prison. I don't know why it is so important to him that Ronald Ryan should die, but I know enough not to suggest that the execution upsets me. Nevertheless, my lack of proper enthusiasm irritates Dad. He tells me that Ronald Ryan shot a prison guard in the back of the head, even though the prison guard begged for mercy. It was the act of a cold-blooded, heartless maniac. Unwisely, I ask how he knows that the prison guard had begged for mercy. 'Because he would of!' Dad says. 'Of course he would of! If someone's going to shoot you in the back of the head, you beg for mercy! Jesus Christ! Do you think he *didn't* beg for mercy? Of course he did!'

Dad keeps up the rant. He doesn't bother much with evidence to support his assertions. He says that prison is 'a laugh' in a country like Australia. There are men in prison who'd raped and murdered tiny children, and what are they doing? Listening to radios, wolfing down three square meals a day, even doing university courses if they want to, some of them. What should happen to them is that they should be chained to the wall twenty-four hours a day.

It's his vehemence more than anything else that makes me certain he's wrong. And it's the first time I have ever felt that my father is truly wrong about something. I hate to think of this stuff whirling away inside his head. He's not a violent man. Where does it come from?

Prison

THE ONLY OBVIOUS way to cross over into Pakistan was to walk. I knew the direction and headed off. Before I'd made it to the outskirts of the city – just desert and a few houses that looked as if they had been fashioned by hand from the very earth on which they sat – I was hailed by a policeman. Confident enough about dealing with cops after my sessions with Rasheef in Shiraz, I wandered over for a bit of a chat. The cop wanted to see my passport. I wasn't sure he was allowed to do that, but I co-operated nonetheless. He glanced at the pages, seemed unable to make much of it and handed it back. But there was clearly something about the look of me that he couldn't quite enjoy. He called over another cop, who wanted to know, so it seemed, where I thought I was going. 'Pakistan,' I said. This confirmed their doubts about me; I was heading in the wrong direction. They took me along to a booth in the market where a more senior cop was able to confirm the suspicions of the two junior guys. My visa was way out of date.

By this time, a dozen cops were on my case, mostly being nosey. It was a break in the monotony of these barren backlots of the nation to catch a visa sneak who was so close to making a clean getaway. The senior cop locked up the booth, clapped handcuffs on me and had the juniors form a guard. I was marched through the market with four rifles aimed at the seat of my green trousers. The citizens were full of curiosity and kept stopping the march to ask the senior cop questions, which he seemed only too happy to answer. I tried to look both menacing and harmless.

The drama of the occasion thrilled me and I wanted to look like a vile fugitive – but also like a harmless kid who'd slipped up in some forgiveable and forgettable way. It was difficult for me. The cop who was carrying my suitcase was about my own age in a uniform that was too big for him. He kept glancing down at my pointed shoes with undisguised delight. During one of the pauses we made for the big cop to skite to the locals, I whispered to the boy, 'Beatles!' He put down the suitcase, and with a huge grin acted out a Ringo-esque trip on air timpani.

Zahedan was a slow and sleepy old town in every respect, except when it came to the dispensing of justice. I was in front of a magistrate within a half-hour of apprehension. My guess was that I would be fined. And my further guess was that I would be let go, or simply tossed over the border into Pakistan, when it was revealed that I had no money to pay the fine. I was almost certain that barter would not be acceptable, and had no plans to line up my wardrobe for the magistrate.

The big cop made a long-winded presentation to the magistrate, a portly middle-aged, jovial man with a ludicrous toothbrush moustache. The magistrate cheerfully satirised, with raised eyebrows and exaggerated expressions of dismay, the bombast of the big cop. He fined me a very small sum and offered me a little toy salute of farewell. Alas, the next case had to be interrupted when the big cop learned that I had no money to pay the fine. The magistrate, with more sorrow than conviction I think, sentenced me to five months in the slammer – a month for each ten rials I was unable to provide. He gave me a look that said, 'Kid, my hands are tied.' I smiled to show that there were no hard feelings.

My fingerprints were taken in a small, busy office down the hall, an office indistinguishable, I imagine, from police offices all over the world: paperwork everywhere, a couple of typewriters, portrait of a big shot on the wall (the Shah, in this case), a half-dozen adipose policemen shuffling about. My arrest had dramatic integrity: the right actors, the right props, the right lines. And this integrity was enhanced by the fingerprinting. Two sets of prints were taken; one for the locals, the other for Interpol. The Interpol set was taken on finer quality paper, with a Paris address printed at the top of the sheet. I was thrilled. *Me*, Bobby, Frank Hillman's son from Eildon, Victoria, Australia, Nowheresville, a butcher's apprentice, now being fingerprinted for *Interpol*!

The procedural care befitted a sombre induction, a ritual initiation into a braver, broader, more dangerous, much sexier world. The fingerprint cop took each finger and firmly rolled it on the ink pad, then on the allotted squares on each of the sheets. His deftness filled me with admiration. He knew what he was doing. On the Interpol set, he took even greater care, down to spelling my name correctly in the data blanks. The completed Interpol sheet looked like a certificate, something that commended both the print-taker and myself. I was proud of it, and I'm sure the cop was, too.

Approaching the prison at Zahedan was like viewing a walled medieval city revealed by careful excavation. Drifts of fine grey sand climbed the stone walls to about half their height. Squat towers along the walls looked over the flat desert plain. Just one barely defined road ran to the prison, straight to the gates. The place seemed lifeless in the shimmering heat haze, but once the prison bus drew closer the black silhouettes of guards in the towers became distinct. The dozen or so other prisoners in the bus, all chained like me with cuffs and ankle irons, did not bother to study the looming city. It was pride, I suppose. They knew the punishment in store for them and didn't wish to bestow on the place the bleak compliment of an anxious glance ahead.

As soon as we were inside the walls, my assumption of superior treatment likely to be afforded to a cheerful white boy proved perfectly sound. The other prisoners, all Iranians, were bullied onto a stone square in the blazing sun to await the pleasure of the authorities. My cuffs and leg-irons were removed and I was permitted to sit against a wall in the shade. A naked prisoner, bathing himself at an ancient fountain in the square, called raucously to me and shook his dick. He was immediately slung by his hair to the ground by an incensed guard, then kicked in the backside all the way to a small, sinister-looking hut at the back of the square. While my fellow new arrivals wilted in the sun, rag bundles at their feet, I was served a cup of tea by a guard with a vile-looking length of cane under his arm, its tip frayed into a fringe.

Nothing at all happened for an hour or more, except that I was served a second cup of tea and a glass of chilled water with a diced lemon floating on top. The prison was silent. A long way off, small domed buildings like igloos of mud clustered around two larger, square buildings, similarly made of mud. The heat of the day was so intense that the guards in the towers had cradled their rifles in the crook of an arm, using the free hand to fan themselves with round, wicker paddles. The new arrivals, out in the sun, stared straight ahead or occasionally lifted their hands as far as the chain would allow, then dipped their heads to brush the sweat from their eyes. One man whose chains allowed a little more latitude had managed to get a rag or handkerchief settled on his head, but it was soon snatched away by a guard.

My suitcase had been left against the wall, not far from where I sat. Growing bored, but not sure how much liberty I was to be given, I sauntered over to the case, opened it, and exchanged my shoes and socks for my thongs. I wasn't reprimanded. I took out a Nero Wolfe detective novel I'd been saving for a rainy day, sauntered back to my spot in the shade and began reading. Content at first, I gradually considered the resentment I might excite in the other new arrivals. I carefully slipped the Nero Wolfe into the back pocket of my trousers, got to my feet and stood erect. This gesture of solidarity was spoiled when a guard brought me a chair. It wasn't just any chair; it was an upholstered armchair. I demurred politely. The guard, smiling beautifully, insisted. I sat down.

In the middle of the afternoon the guards unlocked the shackles on the new arrivals. Prayer rugs were handed out. The amplified wail of a muezzim echoed about the prison walls. The new arrivals knelt and prayed. In the distance I could see men in their hundreds praying outside the mud igloos. The guards in the towers had disappeared below the parapet. The guards in the square prayed, all clustered together in the shade of the wall. Well aware, after months in Iran, that nothing would be made of my demeanour during prayers so long as I remained respectful, I sat watching silently. At the conclusion of prayers, the guards chained the new arrivals again. The area they occupied had gradually fallen into shade. The guards moved them a few yards so that they were once again in the sun.

Late in the afternoon, I was served a plate of spinach and eggs, together with a fresh round flap of bread, more tea and another glass of cold water and lemon. The spinach and eggs were spiced with paprika. The tea was spiced with cinnamon. I had never eaten anything so delicious, never so relished the taste of tea, the coolness of water.

It was only when I'd finished and my tray had been collected that I gave proper thought to the prisoners who'd arrived with me. They had not been fed, and it was pretty obvious that nothing would be offered to them. Even this late in the afternoon, the heat of the sun was fierce. I decided that I would refuse all further food and drink while my comrades were left baking. I tried to show with compassionate glances what was in my heart, but they didn't look at me at all.

At evening prayer the unshackling and reshackling procedure was repeated. I noticed that most were taking the opportunity to snatch a bit of rest. The oldest prisoner, a bent and seamed man perhaps in his seventies, took quite a time to get back on his feet. An argument broke out between two of the prisoners and two guards. It looked as if the prisoners were calling for the guards to take it easy on the old guy. No blows were dealt out, and the guards took away his leg-irons and allowed him to wait on his knees. A little later, one of them brought him a glass of water. Later still, all the new arrivals were given a drink from metal ladles held to their lips by the guards. By this time I had given up on my vow of solidarity. I was well into the Nero Wolfe.

A huge white moon had risen in the fading blue sky over the desert. A fat little fellow in a grey civilian suit toddled along with a clipboard under his arm, and in an infinitely weary manner whispered a word now and again to the guards. One prisoner, then another, was led off to what would be his home for a good many years to come. I was the last prisoner to be dealt with. The fat guy (I later came to know him as the brother-in-law of the deputy governor) became positively jaunty when he considered my case. He spoke a bit of English and was keen to make use of it.

'Mister Eelamuh? Mister Eelamuh, this is sad days for you, I think.'

'Yep.'

'Why you not pay this monies and go away in Pakistan?'

'I haven't got any money.'

'No monies? No rials? German marks or excetra?'

'Nope. Nothing.'

'Hmm. Sad days for you.'

He must have thought I was stubbornly concealing rials or marks somewhere, because he launched into a warning about the type of people I would meet in prison.

'These men killing peoples. These men using the drugs. Very very bad, all these men. Maybe killing you! Maybe. Very bad in Zahedan for boys. Very bad. Very bad for English chaps.'

'I'm Australian,' I said.

'Very bad for Australian. Only nice for Irani people in Zahedan. Maybe one of these men kill you! Big knife!'

He made a skewering sound as he acted out a stab in the region of the stomach, delighting the guards. I could see that it would be in my best interests to look spooked, even though I found it impossible to imagine anyone stabbing me. I cowered a little, and gulped. Fatty looked pleased, in fact much more than pleased, and the guards seemed to endorse the good sense I'd shown in quailing so convincingly.

'Ha ha!' Fatty laughed. He tousled my hair. 'Nobody stabbing you! Ha ha! I put you in nice place.'

And he did. He sent me to a large, comfortable cell, more like a bungalow, nestled against the eastern wall. The windows were without bars and the door wasn't locked. It was occupied by five men. None was in prison dress, and one wore Western clothing; all looked healthy and well fed. I was introduced by the senior guard who'd escorted me. The prisoners listened languidly without rising from their beds. The cell was illuminated by two upright lamps draped with gauzy red scarves that tinged the whole interior a restful pink.

A bed had been made up for me. The sheets looked fresh and clean. I sat on the bed and smiled winningly at my new comrades. They were full of curiosity once the guard had departed, and squatted around me to ask questions. The prisoner in Western clothes soon took over the interview. He introduced himself as Mushtaf, not an Irani but a Pakistani, and he spoke perfect English. He wanted to know (both for himself and on behalf of my other four cellmates, so it seemed) what I had done to get myself arrested. I had overstayed my visa, I explained. My new comrades guffawed or else smiled politely. The gossamer quality of my infraction seemed to them, I guessed, too ludicrous for words.

'You are very welcome among us,' Mushtaf said. 'With your leave, I will introduce my friends.'

Each prisoner bowed just a little as his name and his infringement was mentioned. Ali, about fifteen, had cut his uncle's throat, his uncle being a very bad man ('horrid' was Mushtaf's term). Older Ali, in middle age, very shrewd about the eyes and wearing a beard more carefully barbered than was usual amongst Iranians, had been shafted by his wife's family over something to do with heroin. Then came a bald, chuckling little man who was introduced as Peter, with no explanation of the name given. Whatever Peter's crime, it was evidently too awful to talk about, because Mushtaf moved on with a grimace and a 'you don't want to know' gesture of his hand. Hossein, the fourth of my cell-mates, was the only one who exhibited the proper *fuck yez!* manner of a genuine bad guy. In Australia, he would have ridden with the Banditos. His face was battered, his nose was a mess, and half his upper lip had been reduced to a thin, taut scar. He relished the opportunity to mime his crimes when Mushtaf spoke of them, lassooing his own ankle with his scarf, drawing it tight, then sticking out his tongue to demonstrate the rigour of strangulation.

Mushtaf didn't mention what had caused *him* to be detained with these other desperadoes. He kept himself a little aloof without actually disowning his pals. He looked to me the least candid of the lot. (I was not without some powers of diagnostic insight.) And he seemed to be held in slight contempt by the others. They made faces behind his back, as if he were a fraction too la-de-da for his own good.

Older Ali made breakfast the next morning: cheese, bread, tea. The cell was equipped as a self-contained dwelling, with a stove, a small refrigerator, cooking utensils. An electric fan kept it cool enough. I knew that these conditions would not apply throughout the whole prison, but I kept my questions for later.

I offered to pay my way with books, but was refused. Mushtaf, however, was thrilled to bits with my library. He broke into tears when he found a couple by Evelyn Waugh. 'Here now, you have made me a very happy fellow, Robert. I have had nothing to read for six months. English novels simply don't come our way.' He settled down for the entire morning with *Put Out More Flags*, ignoring the jibes of Hossein, who showed what he thought of novels by rubbing *Eros and Civilization* along the crack of his bum.

It was only when Mushtaf had finished the Evelyn Waugh that he became talkative again. 'I was sure you would ask me that question before long,' he said, responding to my query about the privileges of our cell. 'The fact of the matter is that we all have private resources. Otherwise we would suffer the fate of our brethren across the way.' He gestured, indicating the rest of the prison. 'But you mustn't imagine that this spares us every sort of calamity. Hardly. We shall all hang.'

'What?'

'Oh yes. You mustn't look so shocked. We shall all hang, by and by.'

'But how come?'

'The law, my dear young friend, the law. What other explanation could there be? The law.'

The others seemed to know what Mushtaf was talking about, and confirmed his prediction with good-natured shrugs.

I didn't quite believe what Mushtaf had told me. But on the way to the fountain to wash myself later in the morning, Mushtaf keeping me company, I put good manners aside and asked if the sentences were likely to be delayed for a while yet.

'Yes, for some years. Two years for me, I would hazard. For Hossein, many years yet. He is very wealthy, and his family is very wealthy, too. Ali, two months only, when he comes of age.'

'How can you bear it?'

'My dear young friend, it is our common fate. You may die before me, for all I know. Perhaps from cholera when you reach Pakistan. Do not drink water in the villages. In the cities, sit in the lounge of a big hotel and ask a waiter for a glass of water. He will think you are a guest. But wear proper shoes, not these things, what are they called?'

'Thongs.'

If Younger Ali were to be hanged in two months, I would still be in the prison. I felt uncomfortable – not nearly as uncomfortable as Ali must have been feeling, but uncomfortable all the same. I was incapable of imagining that life for anyone could reach such a dire conclusion as death on the gallows. No matter what I read of the awful ways in which a life might end, and of the despair of people who know that the end is coming, perhaps in a frightful form – still I didn't believe it. In fact, I barely believed in death at all. The world was made of feathers. When I saw the little haulier crushed in Istanbul, the feathers blew away, but only for a time. Every disaster could be averted, every fall would be cushioned. People who were starving to death would find food before it was too late. Those flailing in the water, unable to reach the shore, would be rescued. It was not that I was absurdly optimistic. I was simply absurdly conceited. A cheerful, well-mannered white boy would not come to a bad end – the world would not allow it. And this vanity went so far as to overrule the lessons I might take by looking about, east and west.

This conceit is a mystery to me, even now. I hadn't grown up as a pampered princeling. Vicious domestic arguments had raged around me; friends would come to school with black eyes and split lips when their dads were on the warpath; my own father would sometimes go berserk, rearing above me with a war souvenir samurai sword, whispering that he was about to cut off my head. I had seen my mother and then my stepmother sobbing inconsolably over the wretchedness of it all. I had seen children pulled mottled from the lakes and rivers of my home town, dead forever. I had woken in the wreck of a big black Humber with other children, alive a few seconds earlier, now torn apart. But I would not believe any of it. Ali would not hang.

Wives appeared in our cell the next day. They tidied it up, swept the floor, put food on the shelves, presented children to their dads for a kiss and a cuddle, then departed, like shadows. Mushtaf, who had no wife, put *Vile Bodies* aside and took me out for a tour of the prison. I had seen only a few of the prisoners from 'across the way' up close. I didn't know exactly where they were kept. I didn't know anything about their conditions. The guards greeted Mushtaf courteously and he responded with a smile and a nod, like a sympathetic noble touring a slum. Beyond a barracks, we came to a village within the prison – round mud huts, a number of larger mudbrick buildings, crude concrete structures that looked like man-made caves. The only apertures in the buildings were the small doors, each fitted with broad, hinged wooden slats, which now swung ajar.

At the sound of our approach, prisoners began to emerge from the huts and caves. All were dressed in raggedy prison calico; most wore a small cap like a kipar on the crown of the head. They ranged from boys in their mid-teens to wrinkled and stooped old men. They squinted in the fierce light, holding a hand above their eyes. There were no fat prisoners, and a few were almost as thin as the emaciated figures I'd seen emerging from death camps in old newsreels. They stared at me with amazement or suspicion, these true prisoners. Some of the boys thrust themselves forward and studied me boldly, aggressively. Others backed away, averting their eyes. A few older men seemed perfectly aware of who I was and what I was doing in the Zahedan lock-up. Mushtaf spoke with them pleasantly, and they salaamed and shook my hand. One of them ushered me towards a mud igloo in the manner of a conscientious host.

I bobbed my head to enter the hut and, after my eyesight had adjusted to the darkness, I saw a dozen men squatting around a large earthenware bowl. They were eating from the bowl, using one hand in that dexterous Middle Eastern way to deftly fold strips of bread and scoop up a mush of watery yoghurt. A space was quickly made for me at the bowl; one man after another appealed to me to accept the best of what was left. I took some bread, made it wet and swallowed it down. To take more seemed disgraceful – the men were so ill-nourished that even the small amount I ate might leave a big gap in their guts – but to refuse them when they so insisted would be even worse, maybe. I took some more bread, then mimed a full tummy.

From hut to hut we went, and at each I accepted bread and mush. In one hut a young man, full of disdain, appalled his comrades by demanding to know what I thought I was doing in Iran.

'He asks why you are here,' Mushtaf translated.

'In jail?'

'No, unless I am mistaken, his question has to do with your reasons for coming to Iran at all.'

'Just to see things, tell him.'

'I rather doubt he would understand that.'

'Tell him I was working in Shiraz and now I'm going to Pakistan. I mean, when I get out of jail I'm going to Pakistan.'

Mushtaf translated. The young man jerked his head in contempt. He hissed something rapidly, gesturing towards me as he spoke. The other prisoners remonstrated with him, none so angrily as an old, legless man who shouted up at him from the dirt floor. 'He says you are a fool,' Mushtaf explained quietly once we had left the hut. 'He is a man who hates tourists. He is of the opinion that Westerners come here to laugh at the sorry state of the country. They will shoot him soon, I fear. Pay no heed. His manners need mending.'

At the back of the prison compound we came to two huts with their wooden gates still locked. It was possible to make out faces in the gloom within. Mushtaf spoke quietly through the wooden slats. A guard standing nearby gestured for a cigarette. I had a packet that Older Ali had given me. I lit one for him, and handed him two more. A clamour erupted. Hands reached through the slats. I was about to pass the remainder of the packet to the men, but the guard stood in front of me and shook his head. Mushtaf shepherded me away.

'What's wrong?' I asked.

'The prisoners are not permitted to smoke.'

'But we smoke.'

'But not the other prisoners. Especially not those being punished. You cannot flout the rules, Robert.'

'Are they being punished, those men?'

'Yes.'

'What did they do?'

'They are in jail for smoking opium. They must stay there until they repent. Then they will be sent elsewhere. It is very distressing for them.'

We visited the barracks. Off-duty guards, who were in fact soldiers, sat around long wooden tables, taking it easy. They seemed happy enough to see Mushtaf, whose manner changed to suit the rougher society. He joked with them, nodding toward me as if I were his idiot nephew. The guards laughed with him, sometimes glancing at me satirically. One beefy man, shirtless, strolled over and struck a body-builder pose in front of me. He took my hand and slapped it on the raised muscle of his arm. The other guards laughed loudly, and laughed again when Mushtaf gave them what I took to be an account of my shock and dismay on learning that my cell-mates were to be hanged. The beefy guard, a man of fine comic temperament, circled Mushtaf's neck with his huge hands, pretending to lift him towards heaven. Mushtaf joined in by sticking his tongue out and rolling his eyes.

The tour next took us to the prison kitchen, which was really a bakery. Two mud-brick ovens were fired up, with flat discs of bread being shoved in and out on long, wooden paddles. So far as I could see, the bread strips and watery yoghurt were all the proper prisoners were likely to be fed. The kitchens seemed to be a haven for cripples, with most of the staff blighted in one way or another – missing limbs, a missing hand, a baker with a large healed-over chunk missing from the back of his head and one shoulder. I was offered pieces of meat – kid – being prepared for the guards. A big, lazy dog, as skeletal as the prisoners, followed me about with his tongue lolling out, and sat on my feet whenever I stood still.

A boy of about nine or ten with his head shaved almost bare scrubbed the concrete floor with a bristled brush, using sand from one bucket and water from another. Whenever he bumped up against one of the other kitchen workers, he would stop work and slump back on his haunches, waiting for the occupied spot to be vacated. He looked exhausted and ill. He didn't pay any attention to me until he caught sight of my thongs when I pushed the dog away. Then he looked up at my face. His eyelids fluttered, as if he were about to faint.

Back in the rich folks' cell, I lay on my mattress with my face to the wall. The tour had left me in a state not exactly of shock but of ugly amazement. Looking back at myself, pole-axed by all the unpleasantness around me, I feel like whispering to that trembling form, 'Poor baby! Did all the hungry people upset you?' Because it is difficult to avoid irritation with people like me who, despite knowing what winter is like, wander off into the woods with a pocket handkerchief for a pillow and half a packet of Twisties for sustenance. And my annoyance goes further. I want to use the words that my father might have used, without much in the way of variation: 'Be a man! Who's getting hanged here, you or them?' Or maybe just, 'Ah for fuck's sake!'

As the days passed, I became steadily more aware of the prison's régime of contempt for its captives. A man went mad one day, and ran stooped and squawking around the courtyard, like a chicken fleeing the axe. When he was caught, he was kicked and then picked up and thrown through the air by four guards, who then picked him up and threw him again, returning him to his cell in instalments of three or four yards. I saw the boy who cleaned the kitchen floor hauled howling to the fountain, stripped and scrubbed with his own bristled brush. An old man carrying an earthenware bowl of bread and yoghurt fell in a narrow place; the guards made him lie on top of the spillage so that prisoners had to walk on him as if he were the ground.

The prisoners took care to tread lightly, but I could see no sense in such captious cruelty. Later in life, I read of the response of a former SS officer who was asked why Jews leaving trains at death camps were sometimes harried with whips and dogs, when they could have been efficiently hastened to the huts with mere commands. The officer said that brutality from the outset ruled out reflection. No seed of sympathy should be permitted to put down roots. The culture of the Zahedan prison seemed to be guided by a single maxim: Imagine nothing.

My comrades in the rich folks' cell faced life as you would face a wall. The wall's features had become deadeningly familiar, but at least you had something to stare at, a limit to vision. Mushtaf read his way through my library; Older Ali sang hymns in a murmurous tenor; Hossein squeezed lemons, scores of them each day, catching the juice in a big, brass jug; Younger Ali slept face down on his bed all day and all night; Peter built little log cabins out of his collection of ball-point pens.

One day as I was reading on my bed with my hands supporting my chin, Younger Ali suddenly awoke from his torpor, bounded across the room and erected his forearm in front of my face. He was grinning ear to ear.

'He wants to arm wrestle with you,' said Mushtaf, rousing himself from his reading.

'Arm wrestle?'

'Yes. You know?'

'Oh, arm wrestle. Sure.'

Beside himself with excitement, Younger Ali braced himself beside my mattress, gripped my hand and shouted something that probably meant, *'Comin' at yuh!'* We struggled, we strove, I won. Because although Ali was a muscley little guy, I had spent all the years from age nine to sixteen chopping wood back home. We had a wood fire, the only source of heat in winter, and all the fuel came from the hills. The favoured wood was red gum, a true bastard to split. So there was some steel in my skinny frame, mostly in my arms and shoulders.

We wrestled again; I won again. By this time, the interest of the others was roused. They sat around, delightedly puzzled that I should reveal a talent of this sort. In the third round, Ali dug as deep as he could go. His face, a hand's breadth from mine, glistened with joy. He was completely happy, even in defeat. After losing again, he jumped to his feet and ran around the cell, bouncing off beds and flinging his arms wide in mid-air. Returning to the battle, he grabbed my face and kissed me on the forehead, on the lips, on the chin, wherever he could.

By his sixth straight loss, he was delirious, and the others began to look concerned. They tried to restrain him, but he shrugged them off wildly. I thought that maybe I should simply let him win, but by this time throwing a round would look bad. We wrestled a seventh, eighth, ninth time. The joy in Younger Ali's face had undergone a change. He was still happy, but some partition of the mind that separates fun and fever was about to give way. By the look of his swelling eyes and his teeth more bared than smiling, I thought he might attack me. But he didn't attack. He fell onto his knees and bayed, his eyes rolling back into his head. Hossein and Older Ali put their arms around him and comforted him, whispering into his ear, kissing his cheeks. He was put to bed, and he stayed there for the next two days or so, motionless and silent.

Experimentally at first, seeing what I might get away with, I walked about the prison by myself. The guards took little notice. They had seen the favoured treatment I had been given. They probably thought I had someone's approval. I didn't dare visit the huts for fear that the prisoners would give me their scarce food. I walked about in order not to forget what the prisoners endured. I didn't trust myself to remember. Or perhaps it was not that I feared forgetting, but that I feared the return of self-interest; of the normal dreams and desires that seemed obscene beside the suffering of these people.

How little I understood! The human hunger for comfort, for a few little triumphs, will surely exceed the desire for solidarity with the wretched. If I had known then, as I gazed from a little distance at the scrawny prisoners standing motionless in the sun, how soundly my sympathy would sleep; known how many overflowing plates I would sit down to in the years ahead; how often I would treat a minor headache with easily purchased pain-killers, settle an upset tummy with Dexsal; how regularly, neurotically, I would fret over tiny moles that I feared might bloom into monstrous cancers, over tiny twinges that might signal a cardiac arrest; how common it would become for me to travel the aisles of a supermarket lazily choosing a second and a third and a fourth flavour of fruit yoghurt; how unthinkingly I would voice my disdain for the soulless society of my own country that offered most of its citizens nothing but a quality diet, reliable medical care and shelter from the weather – if I had known this, I would have been sickened. But I was sure that I would remember, if I stared hard enough.

I walked all over the prison, repeating softly 'Don't forget, don't forget, don't forget'… but even as I spoke those words, I dreaded seeing something bad – a prisoner being beaten or humiliated, the unconcerned gaze of the guards at the plight of some crippled old codger struggling to get up from his prayer mat. And I was well aware of the luxury I enjoyed – the luxury of knowing that I would leave the prison.

It was while I was trapped in this way with my bad conscience that I was compelled to deal with a new dilemma. Older Ali wanted to have sex with me. He asked politely, through Mushtaf. I said no, and Older Ali thanked me graciously for at least having considered the idea. Then he came back with a new proposition. Would I be willing to provide something that stopped short of full-on sex? Again, I said no. But the more I thought about it, the more I questioned my reluctance. The man was going to hang. What would it matter if I used my hand in a mechanical way to introduce into Older Ali's blood – the blood that ran such a troubled, gallows-haunted course – a little spice? I could do fuck-all else for any of these people who had taken me in and treated me so generously.

But then, what of all the others in the cell? I had months of my sentence left to run. I might emerge into freedom at the end of my stint shagged senseless. Or I might find myself converted willy-nilly to homosexuality. That was something I dreaded. If I became homosexual, I would no longer be able to dream about naked women. A centre-fold would mean nothing to me. The breasts! The breasts, in particular! How would I ever cope if I lost my longing to nuzzle into a warm pair of breasts like a kitten settling on a cushion? To satisfy Older Ali, I would have to bid farewell to a richly agonising fantasy life. And I'd have to put up with moustache kisses, like those that Mister Ali had planted on my cheeks and neck back in Kuwait. Also, it had not escaped my notice that men didn't always smell all that good.

In the end, I lied. I told Mushtaf to announce that I was forbidden by my religion to engage in sex before marriage, with either men or women. And my church held to a very strict interpretation of sex. Touching, kissing, fondling of any sort were completely out of the question. Before Mushtaf made this announcement, he wanted to know, just out of curiosity, what church I was talking about. Maybe he doubted my sincerity – I didn't know.

I tried to think of the most abstemious denomination I'd ever heard of. Methodists were fairly severe, so far as I knew. Baptists – they were against a lot of things. Seventh Day Adventists? I knew they were weird, but maybe they had some odd rule that permitted pre-marital sex, like the Mormons. Anglicans I knew about. Churchy Goward in my home town was an Anglican vicar. He was a very tall man whose stoop gave his body the appearance of being hinged in the middle. He would stiffen into an upright posture with an all-but-audible clang at the first sniff of quite ordinary sin. He had once asked a woman wearing red lipstick to leave the church in the middle of a christening, so it was said. But then there were the Catholics, famous for their taboos, *very* famous for them. I came down on the side of the Catholics. 'I'm a Catholic,' I said. 'Roman Catholic.' Of course, at that time I didn't know that if you actually *wanted* your trousers plundered, the Anglicans and Catholics were the first people you would turn to.

It was settled. As I'd learned, the Muslim attitude to the infidel was essentially one of pity for the benighted. They weren't about to ask me to risk the wrath of God for the sake of a roll in the hay. Older Ali seemed to approve my piety, patting my head and nodding sympathetically. Mushtaf remained sceptical, but kept it to himself. I felt awful, as I ought. To compensate, I worked up an insane enthusiasm for the hobbies of my pals. I helped Peter erect a skyscraper from his carton of dud ball-points. I put in a two-hour shift with Hossein on the lemons. I taught Younger Ali, who had no hobbies, the craft of paper aeroplane construction, decorating the wings with green crescents, little Iranian flags and tiny depictions of the Shah saluting. But never an hour passed without me squirming over my sexual parsimony.

We saw very little of the prison bosses. Fatty hadn't shown himself since I arrived. I saw senior guards once in a while, but nobody who looked as if he had any real command. Then one day, without warning, the guards began sprinting all over the prison, rallying the inmates to an open-air address from the chief himself. I tucked in my shirt, put on shoes and socks in place of thongs and lined up with the rich folk, a little to the side of the other inmates in the courtyard. The guards skittled up and down, shouting at the more decrepit prisoners to get to their feet. When every soul in the prison was facing the front, the captain of the guards thudded up the steps to the top platform of a dais that had been set up outside the administration block. His few quiet remarks were amplified by old Beefy, genius of comedy, in a raspy baritone. I didn't ask Mushtaf for a translation. It seemed likely that Beefy was telling everyone to shut up and stand up straight, and that it would go badly for those who didn't.

One of the standard features of the abuse of power seems to be the exacerbation of wretchedness. If those under your régime are miserable, take whatever occasion you can find to remind them that the calibrations on the rack allow for a little more misery yet. We waited, most much more uncomfortably than me, hour after hour, for nothing. Calls to prayer went by unobserved. The guards themselves looked exhausted. Fortunately, it was not hot – a whimsical breeze had covered the sky with clouds – or some would have fainted in the first hour. After a couple of hours had passed I asked Mushtaf, out of the side of my mouth, what the hell was going on. 'I don't know,' he said. 'Don't talk.'

The hour of the midday meal went by without anybody getting fed. I could look over the entire prison population – row after row of men and boys dressed in ragged calico. The men were not suffering in any obvious way. They were not grimacing or swaying on their feet. But their eyes were blank, like those of tired beasts. It was a bad day – that was all. Many murmured prayers. I noticed two who maintained a degree of defiance. They held their chins high, kept their arms rigid at their sides. It was ironical that strict obedience should show up as defiance, but it did. The undefiant simply held themselves up as best they could, with no show of reserve energy. When the guards passed up and down the rows, they would stop in front of each of these rebels and hand out some small, spiteful punishment, such as pinching the nose and clapping a hand over the mouth to cut off breathing, or rapping with their knuckles on the forehead. One of the rebels let out a yelp when his toes were stomped.

The prisoners seemed to me to have developed an intimacy with boredom. They befriended it, I think, but unlovingly; never admiring it, never offering a compliment. Because it wouldn't go away, they faced it, chatted with it, found a space for it to sit down and grow silent beside them. It was like accepting the company of the village idiot.

To me, boredom was unendurable. I was unpractised. As the hours went by with no appearance by the big chief, I began to seethe with hatred for whoever he was, fashioning reports to be published in important newspapers telling of the stupidity, the incompetence, the *ill-will* of Zahedan prison's top man. Later, I calmed down. I stared at fixed points on the walls, attempted to find rhymes for polysyllabic words (onomatopeia / bring it over here). I held maundering conversations with my father and sister, speculated on the origins of certain superstitions (wishing on an eyelash – where did *that* come from?). I asked myself whether it was fair to add the length of the Missouri River to that of the Mississippi in order to claim the combined Missouri–Mississippi as one of the longest rivers on earth – considering that we in Australia *did not* attempt to add the length of the Darling River to that of the Murray so as to *sneak* into the top five.

Well into the afternoon, when I could no longer ignore all the aches that gather from standing still, I began to yearn for the arrival of the big chief in quite a new way. I wanted him to exist. I wanted him to become a body with a face on top. I wanted him to become a reality. I almost loved the big chief, and if he had appeared I would have wept for the wonder of his being there. It became extremely important to me that there *was* a big chief, a supreme prison authority. I could no longer comprehend the person I'd been a few hours earlier – the person who *hated* the big chief. I wanted to kiss his hand and thank him for being so considerate and kind as to truly be a person at all. *'Oh big chief,'* I prayed softly, *'big chief please, please come!'*

Now and again, with a sound like an armful of kindling dropping to the ground, a prisoner collapsed. No attention was paid. They remained motionless where they fell. Mushtaf began to cry, but very quietly. The two defiant prisoners stood out in relief against the surrounding undifferentiated crowd of faces grown dumb with tiredness.

Finally, with the arrival of evening, the captain of the guard mounted the dais once more. He spoke, and what he said was again bullhorned by Beefy. The prisoners sighed, crooned, and began to move away. The big chief was not coming. Those prisoners who lay on the ground were encouraged by their comrades to rouse themselves. Of the half-dozen or so who'd fainted, all but two were able to make it back onto their feet. Those two were fanned and massaged by their friends, but to no avail. I wasn't able to remain for long enough to find out if they were living or dead.

I think a man becomes a captive only with the passage of time. At first you are a free man detained by idiots, but not a true captive, not a true prisoner. Your vital life is still a savoury complement to the blood that flows around your body. You belong to the true world, not to a sequestered acre of shadows. Your familiar appetites still prod you, still urge you to head north or south for gratification, east or west for a taste of what you crave. But you whack your head on the wall at each imaginative sortie, and you cannot deny the density of the wall you keep hitting. It stands a little inside the other wall, the one you can see.

I was never a captive, of course. My sentence was a joke; the conditions of my imprisonment were a marked improvement on the conditions of my more recent liberty.

And I wasn't slated for the gallows. All the same, I could see what would happen in my head if my sentence suddenly became twenty years, or forever. Most of the people around me were likely to die in this miniature world with its double wall that I would leave soon enough. I could see captivity in their eyes and in the way they walked.

I felt drawn to them. Just the barest welcome into their family had fluffed the hair behind my ears, like a strange, unheralded breeze on a still day. The first smiles that meant anything to me were the smiles offered by these captives. The first kindness that I'd ever appreciated came from these crippled and wearied people offering a share of their bread – or Older Ali gently accepting my refusal to sleep with him. Zahedan prison gave me my first experience of inclusion.

It wasn't to last. One fine day, a visitor arrived at the prison in a Land Rover, and paid my fine. I was called to the office of another prison bigshot. His visitor was a skinny guy with a Kelly Gang beard and more teeth on display than you would have thought the human jaw could accommodate. Once the visitor had been introduced to me as 'also Orzdrea', he greeted me with great cordiality, saying he'd been stocking up in the bazaar when he heard about an Aussie in the clink. He'd come to check me out; thought I might like to see a friendly face. He found out I owed the sheriff here sixpence or something, and paid it. Steve's the name, by the way.

'Thank you very much', I said, miserably, too shocked and disappointed to smile.

'Mister What's-he here says they've been keeping an eye on you, keeping you away from the rough stuff.'

'I've been very comfortable,' I said.

'That right? Reckon you could get a doctor to take a peek at you when you get a chance. Look a bit light-on to me.'

'I have a naturally light build,' I said, offended.

'Well, yeah. But there's light and light, isn't there?'

The prison officer left us to ourselves, perhaps under the impression that we two fellow countrymen might like to embrace and kiss and sing a song. Steve told me all about his business in this neck of the woods. He was an anthropologist from Sydney University, out this way to research a book he was writing on primitive agricultural systems. He went so far as to pick up a piece of paper and a biro from the desk to sketch a shadoof. The warmth of enthusiasm for his subject was like heat from a bar radiator. He was heading up from Pakistan on his way to Tehran, taking the long way round. Hardly anywhere like it in the world, this region, for a proper look-see at the way people used to farm, so he claimed.

An hour after Steve left in his Land Rover, I was standing outside the prison gates with my suitcase in my hand and the pain of a broken heart bruising my ribcage. I'd cried when I'd said goodbye to the rich folks. The rich folks had cried, too. I'd given Mushtaf half a dozen books, including *For Whom the Bell Tolls*, so hard to part with. Older Ali had kissed me on the mouth and crushed my head into his chest. Younger Ali had shyly put my two hands together and enclosed them in his. Hossein had tugged my earlobes.

I AM VISITING my mother in Brisbane. Years have passed since our reunion. There is nothing in my life and relationships to convince my mother that I can be left in charge of my own affairs and she has therefore decided to give me some advice. I know the advice is coming and I am trying to stall it, maybe postpone it forever. I bounce up from the sofa and fetch an ornament from one of the surfaces in the living room laden with such things and return with it to ask questions. Look at this, extraordinary, where did it come from? Or I comment on the strange drama my mother has created with her interior decoration, the dominance of red and black, the placement on ledges and tables of dragon figurines, dozens of them, some pottery, some iron.

But my temporising can't prevail over my mother's determination to save my life. She succeeds in engineering one of those pauses that people of powerful conviction manage so masterfully. A lifting of the chin, a slight pursing of the lips, a hand raised just a little to signal that the bullshit is over.

'You are... restless,' she says.

'Mm.'

'You have a restlessness deep inside you, my little love, deep, deep inside you.'

'Possibly,' I offer, intensely embarrassed and fearing that a Tarot deck might be produced.

'It will not make you happy.'

'No. No, I suppose not.'

'There is a... a hunger in you. A hunger for love.'

'Well. Maybe.'

'I am telling you things that are difficult for you to accept. But you must.'

With anyone else, someone whose feelings I did not have to be quite so careful with, I would have said, 'For God's sake!'

'I have received a letter from − (and here my mother names the mother of my third son). She is very unhappy.'

'Yes, I know.'

'She loves you.'

'I know.'

'Then... why? Why, my love?'

'Restless?' I offer, meekly. 'Like you said?'

'Yes, restless. Now listen to me.'

And my mother goes on to warn me, in terms consistent with the drama of her living room, of all that will befall me if I do not open my arms to love. At times, she comes on like the head of a stern boarding school for boys. At other times, she sounds like a marriage celebrant tendering passages of Kahil Gibram and the Desiderata. And every now and again, she draws her purple and gold shawl close around her shoulders and becomes Madame Sosostra.

Love, she tells me, is not just sex. Do I understand that?

Yep, I reply.

Not too obviously, I hope, I fix my gaze on the framed photographs a little beyond my mother's shoulder. One of the pictures shows her at a square dance with the man who, decades past, succeeded my father in her affections.

'Be very careful,' my mother says, 'with the people who love you. More careful than you've been, so far. That's all.'

After the lecture, I slouch out into the garden to smoke the first of ten cigarettes. I feel exhausted. I stare at the impeccable garden my mother has planted; at the smart, modern house she lives in. For relief, I think of my father, who never owned a house; who worked as hard as any person in the town, for the barest possible reward. I think of the restlessness that directs his attention away from building, from making. He sees himself as a Gypsy, a free spirit, or sometimes as a man born out of his time. He reads novels set in distant ages of manly trial and ordeal; tales of the Crusades, of Agincourt, of the Teutonic Knights. The women he most desires are of a type that may have flourished for a time in the age of the troubadors: women who minister to him tenderly after battles, bind his wounds, sing him songs, disrobe at a word of suggestion and croon at his touch. The women of the green island are essentially dusky versions of this accomplished, uncomplaining, eternally tender strain.

He likes to hunt with a bow and arrow. The bow he uses is unfancy: a lemonwood arc, modelled on the English longbow. He is a good shot. He also fishes, and as an angler he has no peer in my home town. While other fishermen struggle and curse, my father, a few metres downstream from his frustrated comrades, serenely floats a fly over a tiny rippled patch of water he likes the look of and pulls in a rainbow trout. He is also a fine shot with a .22.

The time comes when his restlessness — a great sustaining force in men and women alike — is no longer there. Broken in spirit by the ugly failure of his marriages, he becomes content to sit and drink shandies under an apple tree in the backyard. The doctor has warned him off full-strength beer. Sighing, bitter, he declines into old age, no longer able to long, to yearn. He sells his bow and arrows, his rifle, and barely bothers with fishing.

I drive up to Eildon to visit my father one Saturday towards the end of his life. He's under the apple tree, stretched out on a banana lounge he'd rescued from the dump. Pale, broken, his chin and cheeks stubbled silver, he has roused himself so far as he can to ask questions about my life, my wellbeing.

'Are you happy?' he asks, turning his grey eyes to me. He seems puzzled by his own question.

'Yes,' I say. 'I'm happy.'

He studies my face for a time, perhaps half a minute.

'Well, good,' he says. 'Want you to have better luck than me. But you are happy, aren't you? You're getting along?'

'Yes, I say, I'm happy.'

'Good,' he says. 'I want you to be happy.'

I see that he is crying. The pallor has left his face and it has become charged with a rush of crimson. His lips tremble. I have never before put my arms around my father at such a moment, and I can't do it now. I avert my eyes. 'I'm okay,' he says. 'I'm okay. Bloody sook, I am.'

He picks a cigarette from a packet — not an unfiltered Temple Bar but a timid Wills Super Mild. He has trouble lighting it. His hands are unsteady. Finally he gives up and lets his hand, holding the cigarette, drop to his side. He closes his eyes, breathes in rapidly two or three times, small hiccuping gulps. He opens his eyes again only when he has his tears under control.

'Be happy if you can,' he says, mastering his emotion with an attempt at gruffness. 'Okay? Will yuh?'

# Butcher Shop

I LEFT A trail of clothing, books and DNA on the journey from the border to Karachi. A month on the road, and all that remained of me was a blue shirt, the trousers of my green suit, my thongs, skin, bone and about half the normal complement of blood for a boy my age. The other half had been sold in hospitals along the way, always under the supervision of a fiercely scornful Western-trained woman doctor with thick spectacles worn around the neck on a plastic chain. It couldn't have been the same short-tempered doctor in every blood bank between Lahore and Karachi, but it didn't seem possible for a half-dozen doctors to look so alike.

In one of the most modest restaurants of Lahore I met a couple of insanely gregarious high-school students home from Karachi on holidays. After purchasing my striped shirt with the button-down collar, they furnished me with introductions to relatives down south. The translations read out to me were pure subcontinent rococo, ornamented with such phrases as, 'My tragic friend has met calamity in sundry episodes of ill-fortune.' It made me soaringly confident of the reception I'd be given by the Karachi rellies. One of the letters was addressed to the editor of a newspaper. Just let me hobble into Karachi, I thought, and I'm a made man.

Unfortunately, one further sundry episode of ill-fortune was waiting to test me. On the road to Karachi I contracted dysentery (as it was later diagnosed). Nowadays, a mild pain in the tummy is enough to force me to my knees in prayer, but as a boy I possessed (fluctuatingly) a fortitude that would have awed Prometheus. Riding in racks on the roofs of truck cabins (every truck in Pakistan was fitted with one of these devices, to accommodate the poorest of travellers), I writhed like an eel and was forced at ten-minute intervals to bang on the cabin roof for a rest break. The patience of the drivers was astonishing. They might have roared off down the highway while I was whimpering in the roadside shrubbery, but they didn't. They waited, and helped me remount to the rack when I was done with a sympathetic slap on the tush.

I came to Karachi, burning, burning. The city seethed. Nobody moved but that they darted, and my vision could barely cope with the crying and carolling forms of hurrying people as they teemed along the streets. In near delirium, I prevailed on a man selling handbags to give me a few coins and a black vinyl satchel in exchange for my suitcase. I went with the coins to a pharmacist and purchased an envelope of yellow powder, together with what looked like a ten-year supply of assorted antibiotics doled out with a ladle into a brown paper bag. Taken together, these medicines, so it was promised, would cure almost anything that affected the human bowel. Lacking water, I washed down the powder and a handful of antibiotics with a bunch of feculent grapes, and almost immediately lost all sensation in my body below my chin – a great relief.

My legs still did my bidding, numbly. I wandered pleasantly, asking directions, until I came across the address of one of the people to whom I had been commended by the high-school students in Lahore. The address was that of a dilapidated hotel.

The man I was looking for was, as it turned out, a porter. He was unable to read, but carried the letter excitedly down to the street and called to a friend selling boxed sets of kitchen knives on the footpath. The knife seller read the letter aloud, attracting an audience with the shrillness and delight of his delivery. After a period of passionate dispute involving everyone in the audience, it was decided that I would be found a free bed in the hotel. And so I was, except that the bed was a wooden bench on a drooping rear balcony. A number of bald car tyres and perished inner tubes were stored on the balcony, together with heaps of cardboard cartons holding what I eventually discovered were player piano rolls.

I never saw the porter again. After two days' rest and a lot more medication, I headed off with my black vinyl satchel in search of my other mark, the newspaper editor. Not knowing exactly which way to head, I approached a shoe salesman down in the city. I chose the shoe salesman so that I would have something to chat about if he turned out to be the sort of person who liked a chat. I had sold shoes myself in the Myer Emporium, not so long ago. He was very helpful. He drew me a map on the lid of a shoe box. He seemed to be suggesting that my destination was fairly distant from where we stood, but I was undaunted. This might be the break I was waiting for.

I walked for a very long time. When night fell, I was no longer in the city. The landscape was like an endless vacant lot. Every now and again a traveller going in the opposite direction would pass me and smile. Standing in the darkness and finding only random points of light in the distance to guide me, I was beaten.

I felt like a character in a novel – made to act the fool, to humiliate himself, to hope when hope was ridiculous, to dance like a trained bear – who had turned on the author and cried out, '*No!* You're cruel and heartless and I will never serve you again, *never!*' But I was coaxed out of my rebellion; I listened to the author's cynical blandishments. 'Don't be so hasty, the editor might really be there, might really be waiting for you, might give you a wonderful job with heaps of prestige, might…'

The editor *was* there. He lived in an improbably modern house, one of only four in a pioneer suburb of the Karachi leisured. Lights shone brightly within. I knocked on the door and asked the attractive woman who answered for the man whose name was written in English on the envelope. The man who came to the door – tall, composed, well-dressed – asked courteously if he could be of service to me. He looked up and smiled at me every so often as he read the letter I offered him. 'Come to this address tomorrow morning,' he said, writing on the back of the envelope. 'Wait just a minute.' He returned to what sounded like the laughter and hubbub of guests, and came back with three vol-au-vents on a paper plate.

I slept that night on the grassy bank of what appeared to be a creek, but morning light showed to be an irrigation ditch. I swallowed the remainder of my bag of antibiotics with the last of the grapes, made myself look as beautiful as I could, and went off to find my man, my hoped-for benefactor, my last hope.

The newspaper office looked exactly as newspaper offices look. Scores of people worked in an attractively frantic way at scores of typewriters at scores of desks. At the largest desk my man sat calmly beckoning me. He had no typewriter. In few words, all of them kind, he told me that there was not the slightest chance that I could become employed at the newspaper. He encouraged me to return to my native land, where I would be likely, very likely, to become employed on an English-language newspaper. 'What was my city?' 'Melbourne,' I replied. 'Ah, *The Age*!' he said. 'You will surely find employment at *The Age* newspaper. *The Age* newspaper is a very fine newspaper,' he said. I should go home and speak to the people at *The Age* newspaper.

The medication I had been dosing myself with was acting on my body in a peculiar way. The pain and the urgent need to find a dunny had passed, but a weird listlessness took over. If I stalled any forward movement, even briefly, my knees gave way. If I leaned against a wall, I slid down it. The only remaining opening for employment in Karachi – that of living off my own blood, a sale a week at the hospital – was closed off when, for the first time, the woman doctor with the thick spectacles refused to stick the needle in my arm. 'Young man,' she said censorially, 'go to your consulate. I will not attend you here. You are quite ill – quite ill.'

The mad insistence of the author whose book I seemed to be inhabiting finally relented. Neither the author nor I could think of a feasible alternative to repatriation. And yet I shivered with unease and a sense of appalling failure all the way to the consulate steps. He seemed a creature with a heart like an ice cube, that author. 'It's been fun, it really has, but it's over old pal – over.' Seduced, abandoned, I walked into the consulate, heart aching, and asked to be sent home.

Twelve months had passed since I'd left home in search of the island of women. My family was waiting to greet me at the airport. My father and stepmother, my sister, my stepsisters – they all looked past me when I approached them, still waiting for me to emerge from the ruck of arriving passengers. It was my sister who first recognised me. She burst into tears. My father grabbed me by the shoulders, some fierce emotion working in his face. He was more relieved than furious one moment, then more furious than relieved the next. 'What have you done to yourself? You idiot, you little idiot!' Day-by-day familiarity with my decline had disguised from me the extent of change. I was extremely thin, and had taken on the colour of the bright yellow powder I'd purchased from the Karachi pharmacist.

In the car on the way back to my home town, my father reminded me again and again that Bertie would take me back as an apprentice butcher. I said I would accept the offer, but my heart was too sore to add conviction to my voice. It was evening when we reached the house. I was fed, petted, put to bed. I smoked a cigarette in silence, staring up at the ceiling. My father opened the door to stare at me, shake his head and tell me how happy he was to have me back. My sister put her head in, and began crying again.

Late at night I woke and wept. I couldn't stop the tears. The only thing on earth I wanted was to be back on the steps of the consulate in Karachi. I would not walk through the door and speak to the startled receptionist. I would not sign the document which would translate itself into an SAS ticket to Bangkok and a Qantas ticket to Melbourne. I would walk back down the steps into the city. I would find a job, any job – I would work with a pick and shovel. Later, I would take a ship to Mombasa, a boat to the Seychelles, a dinghy to the island of women.

THE TOWN CEMETERY is sited in bushland close to the banks of Honeymoon Creek. Wattles and eucalypts hem it in on three sides. Mourners who plant bulbs on the graves of their loved ones (daffodils, jonquils, irises) have learned over the years that the tender winter shoots attract rabbits. Wallabies have been known to leap the wire fence. One was witnessed eating flowers left in a vase by a visitor.

Between the cemetery, the creek and the river lies a patch of land on which plum trees, a ragged lemon tree and a pair of hornbeams struggle along in the shade of the yellow box and ironbark. Half-hidden in the tawny phalaris and barley grass beneath the trees you will find, after an earnest search, the red-gum stumps of all old dwelling, together with other fragments — some smothered in blackberry — of the type of house that once stood here, above the Goulburn. A few lengths of weatherboard as fragile as paper lie flattened to the clay. A curved scrap of corrugated iron, all that is left of a water tank, is so brittle that it is possible to poke a stick through it.

These weather-beaten remains were once part of a grocery shop that my grandfather kept for a time in the 'twenties. The town barely existed in those days, and keeping the shop cannot have afforded my grandfather much profit. Conscientious pursuit of what cannot provide reward seems to have been a hallmark of the male members of my family.

The cemetery has always been a pleasant place to me. I like to walk amongst the graves and stop whenever a familiar name invites me to recall that woman, that man, that boy, that girl. 'Pleasant' is not quite the right word. But I enjoy the brief suspension of anxiety and fret that settles on me when I walk amongst the graves and see so many inalterable conclusions to so many stories. Here, editing is done with. The ending is perfect.

Vernon died at fifty-two, mourned by his wife and brother, so the headstone says. I happen to know that no children were left behind to grieve. What more can be said? Vern lived and died, and once taught me how to gut a trout. Terry was overtaken by cancer and was only eighteen. He was a boy who loved to brag, but I liked him. Mrs Cooper lived next door to my family, and suffered a great deal from having a husband who made a career of a bad back, so rarely was he employed and so wearingly did she strive to compensate. Her husband misses her, the headstone says, and so do her sons and daughters.

My father's grave lies between an anonymous weathered monument and a concrete marker with a small, numbered brass plate attached. The number refers you to a name, should you wish to study the shire records. The inhabitant of the grave died poor and alone, one of many reinterred here by the Americans when the rising waters of the lake drowned an even older cemetery down on the river.

The wording on my father's headstone is mine. It was thought proper that I should find the words, since I wrote stories and poems and was attending university at the time of Dad's death. Recalling that I had once ornamented the restaurant menus of the Parki Saadi with quotations from Chekhov, I opted for brevity. 'Francis Edward Hillman' I wrote, on translucent blue air-letter paper, the only blank paper in the house at the time; 'Dearly loved and sadly missed by his family.' The sheet of blue paper was handed to the undertaker. The undertaker relayed it to the mason. The mason inscribed the words on the headstone. I had written the conclusion of my father's life story.

I often drive up here to the cemetery from the city with a friend — maybe a friend from the town who, like me, hasn't lived there for many years now, or maybe someone who is simply happy to get out of the city for a day. Some are touched by the visit, feeling, I think, that I am sharing something that I would surely reserve for the people in my life I cared for most. Some think it weird, or boring, or disturbingly sentimental. One of the visitors says, with a laugh, 'Do me a favour!'

When I visit the cemetery alone — I am alone now — I attempt a chat with my father. I always glance about warily, terrified of being caught mumbling over a grave. The chats are never successful, because while talking I split in two, and one of me watches the other. The one watching is embarrassed by the one speaking, and eventually starts speaking, too. He says, 'For God's sake shut up, the man's dead.' And then I become one person again, a person who has shut up, as he should.

I don't have anything to say today. I wander through the Catholic section, stopping to stare down at a fresh mound of clay. Bunches of flowers are wilting on the hill of pebbly clay. Looking more closely, I see that a small, gold ring is tied to one of the bunches with a purple ribbon. Is it a wedding ring? It's too small for a man's finger. Why, if such a gesture was called for, was the ring not placed in the coffin? Left here, it could be stolen. The ring, exposed to theft, worries me. I place another bunch of flowers over it, to conceal it. I walk away from the grave reluctantly, still troubled.

It's a balmy day, a late autumn day, the blue sheet of the sky barely touched by cloud. Wattle birds, ransacking the shore pines outside the fence in search of buds, shout their harsh, tribal, two-note caw.

I put my hand on my father's headstone, as I usually do before starting back to the city. But I can't empty my mind. I stand beside my father's grave for some time, fretting about the new grave. Finally, I accept that the wedding ring has been left for much the same reason that I would leave a ring on a grave, or book a ticket on an ocean liner. The ring has been left to place its owner in the story of a life — perhaps to be included in some imagined future. I booked a ticket on a ship to install myself in a story that my father had begun in his imagination, and that I had rounded out.

I leave this place of conclusions just as a car pulls in and parks close to mine, under the pines. I know who this is. It is Madge. I haven't seen her for maybe twenty years. I know whose grave she will be visiting. It's in the Catholic section. I stopped at it almost an hour ago, thinking of the boy, Madge's son, who is buried there. I put him in a novel once, with a cavalier disregard for the feelings of his family.

Madge won't have read that book, I hope. She probably won't recognise me. She's carrying a huge bunch of pink chrysanthemums.

'Tracy,' Madge calls to a stout little girl with yellow hair under a red baseball cap on which the words 'Kylie' and 'Fever' are lettered in sequins.

'Get that vase, love!'

Madge is carrying a trowel and a small mat, for some weeding. She has just about reached me. I am standing at the gate, prepared to take my medicine if I have to. Madge, about the age of the ancient pines above us, glances at me and seems ready to trudge past. Tracy has found the vase, and is running towards us.

'Bobby!' says Madge, and her face fills with wonder as she stands staring up at me, chryssies heaped under her chin. 'You're Frank Hillman's boy, aren't you?'

www.summersdale.com